Studying Society

Studying Society is an introductory undergraduate level textbook which helps students to develop study skills as well as an understanding of the principles of social research and how these principles link to social theory.

Studying Society guides students in learning how to formulate questions, look for answers, understand the methods by which information is collected, critically evaluate information sources and communicate the results of their work to others.

Studying Society encourages students to recognise that the study of society involves a systematic and considered approach to the collection and generation of knowledge, that a wide variety of sources can be utilised in this process and that each source has a unique part to play. In developing these skills, *Studying Society* explores the use of both traditional media, and new information and communication technologies.

Throughout the book and accompanying websites, there is an emphasis on applying the problems and solutions presented to 'real world' issues. This involves the use of examples and exercises which are immediately relevant to the undergraduate experience, to everyday life and to the contemporary concepts which are studied by the social scientist.

This coherent and up-to-date text will be an invaluable learning tool for students of any discipline which involves the study of human beings and their societies.

Karen Evans is Senior Lecturer in Sociology at the University of Liverpool. She has taught research methods to undergraduate and postgraduate students for the past ten years, and was previously a researcher in local government and academia.

Dave King is Senior Lecturer in Sociology at the University of Liverpool. He teaches in the areas of qualitative research methods, the sociology of deviance, and gender and sexuality.

Studying Society

The essentials

Karen Evans and Dave King

Routledge
Taylor & Francis Group

LONDON AND NEW YORK

First published 2006
by Routledge
2 Park Square, Milton Park, Abingdon, Oxon OX14 4RN

Simultaneously published in the USA and Canada
by Routledge
270 Madison Ave, New York, NY 10016

Routledge is an imprint of the Taylor & Francis Group

Typeset in Perpetua and Bell Gothic by
Florence Production Ltd, Stoodleigh, Devon
Printed and bound in Great Britain by
TJ International Ltd, Padstow, Cornwall

British Library Cataloguing in Publication Data
A catalogue record for this book is available from the British Library

Library of Congress Cataloging in Publication Data
Evans, Karen, 1961–
    Studying society: the essentials/Karen Evans and Dave King.
        p. cm.
    Includes bibliographical references and index.
    1. Sociology – Study and teaching (Higher) – Handbooks, manuals,
etc   2. Social sciences – Study and teaching (Higher) – Handbooks,
manuals, etc.   3. Sociology – Research – Handbooks, manuals, etc.
4. Social sciences – Research – Handbooks, manuals, etc.   5. Study
skills – Handbooks, manuals, etc.   6. Report writing – Handbooks,
manuals, etc.   7. College student orientation – Handbooks,
manuals, etc.   I. King, Dave, 1947 –   II. Title.
HM571.E93 2005
301'.072–dc22   2005011139

ISBN10: 0–415–35519–2 (hbk)
ISBN10: 0–415–35520–6 (pbk)

ISBN13: 9–78–0–415–35519–3 (hbk)
ISBN13: 9–78–0–415–35520–9 (pbk)

Contents

CONTENTS

Figures

Tables

Foreword

STEVE FULLER

Professor of Sociology, University of Warwick

It is a pleasure and an honour to write the foreword to a book that so thoroughly captures in print the exemplary pedagogical practice that has been a mainstay of the Department of Sociology, Social Policy and Social Work at the University of Liverpool. I write here from both my knowledge of the history of British sociology and my service as external examiner for the department's undergraduate programmes from 2000 to 2003. This combined basis enables me to recognise a department that for a century has remained true to its origins in providing ample opportunity and instruction in how the social sciences may raise the quality of life of the local community and region, while at the same time contributing to more cosmopolitan academic and policy concerns.

I also write at a moment (the UK in 2005) when publications oriented towards the research interests of other academics are officially accorded much greater value than publications aimed at their teaching interests, let alone the interests of the wider society who might hope to enrich their lives by studying sociology. Against these currents, Evans and King are to be congratulated – and emulated – for having laid out so explicitly the point and procedure of doing sociology in all its registers, from the selection of theoretical frameworks to judgements about the referencing of other authors. Unsurprisingly, perhaps, this book began life as a web-based resource for students. Its interactive feel and approachability led me to recommend the resource to colleagues and urge its translation into the form in which you now see it.

As someone who tends to write allusively and whose impact is most immediately felt on academic colleagues, I very much appreciate the care Evans and King have taken to appeal to a very broad readership without ever insulting their intelligence. It is much harder for academics to write as Evans and King do than the ease of reading their prose might indicate. Indeed, the ultimate significance of *Studying Society* lies in the maxim that the longer race favours the slower runner. Sociology's legacy is likely to be more lasting among those for whom it appears as an inflection of their everyday lives rather than simply another research fashion or line item on their curriculum vitae. My guess is that once the current 'audit culture' of British academia runs its course, both intellectually and financially, *Studying Society* will remain in successive editions as a classic demonstration of how sociological understanding can contribute to a better society.

Steve Fuller
Professor of Sociology,
University of Warwick

Part I

Studying society

INTRODUCTION

To be successful in higher education depends on developing your capacity for independent, self-directed learning. Whether you have come to university straight from school or via some other route, you will probably have been learning in a more supported environment than the one you will find yourself in now. At university you will be expected to take responsibility for your own learning, to identify your learning needs, to organise your time and to find and use a variety of sources of help. Your lecturers won't be organising and monitoring you in the same way that your teachers probably did and you will have a lot of freedom in terms of time and what to do with it. Don't panic though: students today have access to more sources of help than ever before. The world abounds in books and websites designed to help with your studies. And now you have this book to help you too!

This book began its life in a course that we run for our first-year students in their very first semester. The basic aim of the course is to ensure that students are equipped with the various skills that they need in order to complete their other courses successfully. In planning that course we asked ourselves the question: 'What are the essential skills that students in the social sciences need in order to succeed in their studies?'. In trying to answer that question we looked at our own practices and those of our colleagues and decided that what was needed was an integration of social theory, research methods and study skills so that from the very first first-year essay, students are beginning to practise the craft of the social scientist.

We realised that our students would be developing their skills over the whole of their degree programme and beyond and also that we couldn't cover everything in detail. So we have concentrated on providing a starting point with lots of leads to follow up as and when required and in particular on developing an awareness that learning and studying are skills to be focused on and worked at.

- Do you know how to go about studying society?
- Do you know the kinds of questions that you might ask?

1

- Do you know what sources of knowledge might contain some answers?
- Do you know how to search those sources effectively?
- Do you know how to evaluate any information that you might find?
- Can you communicate clearly with others in writing and verbally?
- Do you know how to make good use of information technology in your studies?
- Do you know how students of society carry out research and discover new knowledge?
- Do you know how to use the work of others and refer to it correctly?
- Do you know how to integrate theory into your work?
- If you have answered 'no' to any of these questions, then this book should be able to help you.

This book is addressed primarily to first-year students on degree programmes in sociology, criminology, social policy, politics, geography, social work, communications/media studies, economics, history, or some combination of these; but many other degree programmes such as medicine, and the various professional courses allied to medicine, also require their students to acquire some understanding of the nature of human society.

Students in later years of their programmes and even, we are afraid to say, postgraduates, may find that this book can help to fill in some gaps in their skills base.

The book is designed to help you to develop effective study skills and to develop an understanding of the ways in which we can carry out research into aspects of human society and how we can use theories and concepts to make sense of what we find there.

As a student of society you will need first of all to be able to formulate questions to direct your study, something which is more difficult than it first appears. You then need to know how to go about looking for answers to your questions that might be available in books, journal articles or on the Internet. In order to assess the validity of any answers that are found, you will need to learn to be critical of their sources and to understand the methods by which those answers were arrived at. And, finally, you will need to be able to communicate the results of your work to others. To be a successful student of society, therefore, requires the development of certain study skills combined with an understanding of the principles of social research and how each of these links to sociological theories and ideas.

We shall have much more to say about society and sociology in due course. For now we want to explain that we are not using the word 'sociology' to refer to the specific discipline of that name but to refer to its basic meaning – the study of human society. So a 'sociologist' for our purposes here is not only someone who is studying for a degree in sociology but is anyone who is studying human society. A sociologist is simply someone who is interested in, and fascinated by, human beings. And, because human beings are inherently social animals, we can't get very far in understanding them without studying the societies and social relationships within which their lives are embedded.

How to use this book

You don't need to read through this book from cover to cover. In fact we hope that you will not do that. Compared to students in the natural sciences, students in the social sciences will have to consult a lot of books. But you will rarely need to read a book in its entirety. That is particularly true of this book, which is designed as a kind of handbook that you can dip into for help when you need it. We suggest that you read the next two chapters which are concerned with thinking about society and thinking about studying. Then you should skim over the remaining chapters of the book so you know what they deal with. You can then dip back into them when you need some help with a particular point.

Chapter 1

Thinking about society

Before we go any further we need to say something about our object of interest – human societies. Human societies are amazing and complex phenomena. It is easy to appreciate our own individuality and contemporary popular culture encourages us to focus on our own personalities and those of others. And yet left to our own devices there is little that we can accomplish. Since you were born you have been dependent on other people in one way or another. At first you had to be fed, clothed, washed and kept warm. Gradually you learnt to do these things and many others for yourself. Importantly you also learnt to speak a language. That is a crucial skill which has enabled you to communicate with others around you and to share in the society and culture that has helped to shape the kind of life that it is possible for you to live.

Before you read any further carry out Exercise 1.1.

EXERCISE 1.1

In order to appreciate how our lives are intertwined with those of others, make a list of all the things you have done today which have only been possible because of something that other people have done.

Can you think of anything you have done which hasn't depended on other people?

Did you remember to include all the people who were involved in the long chain of activities that resulted in your having something to eat for breakfast? Did you remember those who built the building you are living in, the people who made your clothes, your furniture, the people who made this book possible, those involved in the fact that you were able to take a bus to get to your lectures this afternoon, including those who built the roads that the bus ran on. Did you remember to include the people who made the paper and the pen that enabled you to write your list in the first place? We could go on; but the point, we hope, is made – without the activities of millions of people around the globe (most of whom you will never meet and who do not know that you even exist) your day today would have been very different. And we haven't even begun to think about all the people who are now dead but whose behaviour over the ages has had an influence on your life.

Now try Exercise 1.2:

EXERCISE 1.2

Do the opposite of what you did in Exercise 1.1 and make a list of everything that you have done today which has affected *someone else's* life.

In that exercise you probably remembered to include the things you have done that have had an immediate effect on those people you are in actual contact with – you perhaps bought a friend a cup of coffee or lent someone a book or a CD. But did you think about the things you did which on their own did not have a big effect on the lives of others but which have enormous consequences when added to the behaviour of many other people? So your university department won't have lost too much sleep if you had decided to study somewhere else; but if many students had made that decision then your department might have had to close down.

Another example, and one of which we are becoming increasingly aware, is the way in which the cumulative actions of individuals can have massive consequences for our physical environment. Our individual decisions to fly away on holiday, to consume drinks in plastic bottles or cans, and many other decisions that we do not think about, will not by themselves have an effect but when added to the actions of millions of other people will shape the physical environment of people who will be around long after we are dead.

The ability to grasp this interrelationship between our individual lives and those of others at a particular period in history is a characteristic of what the American sociologist C. Wright Mills called the 'Sociological Imagination'.

In the following passage Mills draws attention to two important points which are central to sociological thinking. One is that we all, simply by living our lives, have some impact, however small, on the nature of our society and on history. The second is that our lives are shaped by the nature of the society into which we are born. Take a break from reading now and try Exercise 1.3. This will take a bit longer than the earlier ones.

THE SOCIOLOGICAL IMAGINATION

We have come to know that every individual lives, from one generation to the next, in some society; that he lives out a biography, and that he lives it out within some historical sequence. By the fact of his living he contributes, however minutely, to the shaping of this society and to the course of its history, even as he is made by society and by its historical push and shove.

The sociological imagination enables us to grasp history and biography and the relations between the two within society. That is its task and its promise.

(Wright Mills, 1959: 6)

EXERCISE 1.3

Find someone who is the same sex as you but who is 20 years or so older. Probably the people who you are most comfortable with at university are about the same age as yourself, so you can phone a parent, an aunt or an uncle or other relative if you wish for this exercise.

Ask them to tell you something about their lives when they were aged about 20.

Then write down five ways in which your life now is different from what it would have been like 20 years ago.

Now we want to look in more detail at the word 'society'. In the box overleaf is an extract from a book by the American sociologist Peter Berger, in which he discusses some of the ways in which the term 'society' is used. You will probably find that you are not able to understand this passage entirely; don't worry about that. Learning doesn't take place instantaneously and if you are new to sociological ways of writing you will need some practice before you get up to speed. If you have ever learned to play a musical instrument think back to when you began; you certainly didn't just pick it up and play, you spent long hours practising before you could make a decent sound.

Some of Berger's words may be unfamiliar; do you know what he means by 'collectivity' or 'autonomous entity'? Sometimes words can be defined but that doesn't necessarily guarantee understanding, and if you are familiar with a foreign language you will know that sometimes something just cannot be translated adequately; it has to be understood within the language and culture to which it belongs.

7

SOCIETY

Like most terms used by sociologists, this one is derived from common usage, where its meaning is imprecise. Sometimes it means a particular band of people (as in 'Society for the Prevention of Cruelty to Animals'), sometimes only those people endowed with great prestige or privilege (as in 'Boston society ladies'), and on other occasions it is simply used to denote company of any sort (for example, 'he greatly suffered in those years for lack of society'). There are other, less frequent meanings as well. The sociologist uses the term in a more precise sense, though, of course, there are differences in usage within the discipline itself. The sociologist thinks of 'society' as denoting a large complex of human relationships, or to put it in more technical language, as referring to a system of interaction. The word 'large' is difficult to specify quantitatively in this context. The sociologist may speak of a 'society' including millions of human beings (say, 'American society'), but he may also use the term to refer to a numerically much smaller collectivity (say, 'the society of second-year students here'). Two people chatting on a street corner will hardly constitute a 'society', but three people stranded on an island certainly will. The applicability of the concept, then, cannot be decided on quantitative grounds alone. It rather applies when a complex of relationships is sufficiently succinct to be analysed by itself, understood as an autonomous entity, set against others of the same kind.

(Berger, 1966: 38)

Berger's actual definition of society occurs in the middle of the passage in the box – 'a large complex of human relationships . . . a system of interaction'. There are two words here that need further exploration – 'relationships' and 'interaction'. 'Relationship' is another of those words that we use in our everyday lives – most commonly perhaps today it refers to close personal entanglements with boyfriends or girlfriends.

Here is another exercise for you:

EXERCISE 1.4

You are probably already familiar with computers, the Internet and search engines. (Don't worry if you are not – we will look at them later). Put 'relationships' into a search engine such as Google and see what you get.

Romantic involvements are only one type of relationship and sociologists and other students of society are interested in many different types of relationships: we have relationships with everyone we encounter. As a customer in a shop you have a relationship with the shop assistant, albeit a fleeting one; as a student you have relationships with your fellow students (apart from romantic ones!) and with your tutors; as a son, daughter, brother or sister you have relationships with other members of your family; you, like many students, probably have some form of paid employment and you will have relationships with your work colleagues, your boss and maybe, depending on the type of work, with customers. The next exercise will help you to begin to think about these relationships.

EXERCISE 1.5

Make a list of all the people you have been in contact with today, however briefly. Include people you have been in contact with by email, text or tele-phone as well as people you have actually met face to face. Write down what the relationship is – customer/shop assistant, boyfriend/girlfriend for instance. Now write down something about the nature of each relationship and sort them into categories. Here are some things to think about when doing this:

■ How long does the relationship last?
■ Does it involve you as a unique person or you as a member of a category of persons (student, customer, etc.)?
■ Is the relationship an equal one or does one person in the relationship have more authority or power over the other?

If you have carried out this exercise you have made some important steps in beginning to study society. You have systematically recorded some information about your social contacts and, more importantly, you have begun to analyse, to make sense of them. From a simple list you have begun to classify your rela-tionships according to how long they last, whether they are personal or impersonal and whether they involve inequalities of power or not. These last two aspects of relationships are ones that have been of central concern to sociologists over the years. If you want to develop this exercise further think up as many other ways of describing your relationships as you can and extend your analysis to other rela-tionships (including fictional ones in books or on the television) that you can see in the world around you.

This exercise illustrates an important point:

> When we study society we are studying ourselves, and the world about us.

As Peter Berger put it: 'The sociologist lives in society, on the job and off it. His own life, inevitably, is part of his subject matter' (1963: 33).

That fact means that we have endless opportunities to observe social life and to practise trying to make sense of what is going on. You live in a society and every day you will have experiences on which you can draw in your studies, experiences to which you can apply the concepts and theories that you are learning about as you 'study society'.

We can't emphasise too much the importance of considering the meaning of words carefully and in some detail. This is important in order to be able to communicate clearly with other people. But thinking about the meaning of words is also a crucial stage in thinking about *anything*. As Wright Mills (1959: 212) wrote: 'Look up synonyms for each of your key terms in dictionaries as well as in technical books, in order to know the full range of their connotations. This simple habit will prod you to elaborate the terms of the problem and hence to define them less wordily and more precisely' (see the following Top Tip).

TOP TIP

Buy yourself a good dictionary (or better still, get someone else to buy it for you). You will encounter some unfamiliar words in the course of your studies and you will need to check their meaning. Also a good dictionary is usually a good place to start when you are beginning to think about a new topic for an essay or for a seminar presentation. Even when you think you know what a word means, the dictionary will often give variations in meaning or emphasis which can stimulate some new ideas.

The second word in Berger's discussion of 'society' which we suggested needed further exploration was 'interaction'. If you look it up in your dictionary you will probably find that the definition is something like 'reciprocal action or influence' (and if you are not sure what reciprocal means then you should look that up too). For sociologists 'interaction' is usually shorthand for 'social interaction'. Now, we can't actually 'see' society of course. But we can see social interaction taking place in a variety of social settings and in relation to a number of different social activities that take place within them. So again we need to look at what we mean by the term 'social'. In the box below is Peter Berger's attempt to explain it. Notice how he again begins by distinguishing the sociological from the everyday use of the word.

SOCIAL

The adjective 'social' must be similarly sharpened for sociological use. In common speech it may denote, once more, a number of different things – the informal quality of a certain gathering ('this is a social meeting – let's not discuss business'), an altruistic attitude on somebody's part ('he had a strong social concern in his job'), or, more generally, anything derived from contact with other people ('a social disease'). The sociologist will use the term more narrowly and more precisely to refer to the quality of interaction, interrelationship, mutuality. Thus two men chatting on a street corner do not constitute a 'society', but what transpires between them is certainly 'social'. 'Society' consists of a complex of such 'social' events. As to the exact definition of the 'social', it is difficult to improve on Max Weber's definition of a 'social' situation as one in which people orient their actions towards one another. The web of meanings, expectations and conduct resulting from such mutual orientation is the stuff of sociological analysis.

(Berger, 1966: 38–39)

So society only exists as a complex collection of 'social events' in which people 'orient their actions towards one another'. In other words, their actions are reciprocal. Now we would be faced with a situation of complete chaos if each social event required us to work out afresh how to act towards one another. Of course that doesn't happen; most of the time we live our lives in a routine fashion. We encounter other people in the context of social organisations such as schools, universities, factories or sports clubs. The word 'organisation suggests that what goes on in these places is far from random.

One way in which we can look at such social organisations is to see them as collections of people playing particular *social roles*. We shall look at this concept in more detail later. For now it is enough to point out that it refers to the idea that there are sets of *social norms* or expectations that guide our behaviour in social situations. So to take a simple example: in a school we could consider the roles of teacher and pupil. There are other roles in a school of course but those are the two key ones.

If we go back to Mills' notion of the 'sociological imagination' we can see that it is necessary to situate the social organisations and patterns of social interactions in which we live our lives within society as a whole. We must look at

11

how society is structured at this particular period of history and at how that shapes and is shaped by our interactions with others.

One of the elements of social structure that sociologists have often focused on is the pattern of social divisions that occur within societies. In particular the division into social classes has been an enduring theme in the literature, with ethnic and gender divisions being a more recent focus. We shall look at these divisions again later.

Whilst we are all individuals and no two lives are exactly the same, the 'sociological imagination' encourages us to look at the similarities in the lives of people in similar social circumstances. And in fact when we look at them we often find that the things that will have the biggest influence on our lives are the things that we share with many other people and not the things that mark us out as individuals.

In the box below Peter Berger explores the influence of social class on many aspects of a person's life. Note that when we talk about the influence of class (or gender or any other social attribute) we can only talk of 'likelihood' not 'certainty'. There will always be exceptions.

> One's class position determines the amount of education one's children are likely to receive. It determines the standards of medical care enjoyed by oneself and one's family, and, therefore, one's life expectancy – life chances in the literal sense of the word. The higher classes in our society are better fed, better housed, better educated, and live longer than their less fortunate fellow citizens. These observations may be truisms, but they gain in impact if one sees that there is a statistical correlation between the quantity of money one earns per annum and the number of years one may expect to do so on this earth.
>
> (Berger, 1966: 96)

Another way in which we can try to grasp the way in which our own lives are intimately linked to the society in which we live is to consider the distinction that Mills makes between 'personal troubles' and 'public issues'.

PERSONAL TROUBLES AND PUBLIC ISSUES

Perhaps the most fruitful distinction with which the sociological imagination works is between 'the personal troubles of milieu' and 'the public issues of social structure'. This distinction is an essential tool of the sociological imagination and a feature of all classic work in social science.

> Troubles occur within the character of the individual and within the range of his immediate relations with others; they have to do with his self and with those limited areas of social life of which he is directly and personally aware.
>
> Issues have to do with matters that transcend these local environments of the individual and the range of his inner life. They have to do with the organization of many such milieux into the institutions of an historical society as a whole, with the ways in which various milieux overlap and interpenetrate to form the larger structure of social and historical life.
>
> (Wright Mills, 1959: 8)

No, we didn't understand the word 'milieux' when we first came across it all those years ago either, but if you check your dictionary you should find that it simply refers to our social environment, our immediate social circumstances. One of the examples that Mills gives to illustrate this distinction is that of unemployment. The fact that one person is unemployed is a personal trouble with an obvious effect on themselves and their family. But if we consider the statistics on unemployment for a particular society we can see something that goes beyond the experiences of each unemployed person. We can look at how unemployment rates vary from society to society and even in the same society over time.

In a similar way Mills looks at the case of divorce. To the individuals concerned a divorce is (usually) a distressing life event with considerable repercussions. And again we can look at the statistics on divorce and see how rates vary.

Another classic example comes from Durkheim's famous study *Suicide*. In this study Durkheim looked at the ways in which suicide rates varied across societies, over time and varied between particular groups in the same society. Whilst individual circumstance might explain individual suicides, the social facts of suicide rates needed social explanations.

So, we hope we have given you some food for thought about this thing that we call 'society'. As you can see, it is the very fabric of our lives yet at the same time it is a very abstract and somewhat slippery idea. In the next chapter we will make a start in thinking about how to go about studying this amazing and frustrating beast.

13

Chapter 2

Thinking about studying

Study skills

Study skills are not something that you acquire at the beginning of your degree course and then go on to put into practice – they are skills that you will be developing as you use them during, and indeed after, your course. Universities and their students are becoming more and more aware that apart from the specific subject matter that a student may have studied, by the time they graduate, they will have developed skills that can be applied in many types of employment. They will be able to evaluate evidence, arguments and assumptions, reach sound judgements, and to communicate effectively.

Studying Society is designed to help you to develop your skills in these areas not only as a means of achieving success on your particular course but also to enable you to become effective 'students of society' in the broadest possible sense. The study of society involves a systematic and considered approach to the collection and generation of knowledge, a wide variety of sources can be utilised in this process and each source has a unique part to play. We hope to encourage you to integrate different forms of knowledge and to make links between theory and research. Later we will introduce you to a number of important techniques which you can utilise in the study of society, to a variety of practical skills and their application to study, research and theorising. We won't be concerned with matters that relate to specific academic disciplines but we will be concerned with those skills and abilities that are commonly expected of graduates in most of the humanities and social sciences and in particular with the ability to gather information from a variety of sources, to evaluate evidence, arguments and assumptions and to communicate effectively both orally and in writing.

In an appendix to his book *The Sociological Imagination*, Wright Mills encourages students to develop their 'intellectual craftsmanship' and stresses the importance of 'good workmanship' in the study of society. In this book one of the things we are trying to do is to encourage our readers to view studying society as a craft and to identify and develop the skills needed to practise that craft well.

We will show you how this can be achieved through the use of the traditional and novel technologies and practices addressed in later chapters.

TOP TIP: GETTING HELP WITH STUDY SKILLS

One of the first things you should do is check out what is available in your own college or university. Most higher education institutions today will have a department which is concerned with promoting student learning. It is likely to have a website and to provide courses to help you with your studies. Your department may also provide a course or some other means of promoting study skills. The library is another good source of help. Librarians today do more than catalogue books and stamp them in and out: they have particular expertise in defining information needs and locating information sources.

But now let's get out our dictionaries again and see if we can pin down what this thing called 'studying' is all about. If we look in the *Concise Oxford Dictionary* (8th edition, 1990), the verb 'study' is defined as 'to make a study of'. Looking up the noun 'study', we are told it is 'the devotion of time and attention to acquiring information or knowledge, esp. from books'. The second edition of the *Oxford English Dictionary Online* (which you may be able to access through your university library) tells us that 'knowledge' refers to, 'having information acquired by study or research; acquaintance with ascertained truths, facts, or principles; information acquired by study; learning; erudition'. Picking up another keyword from the definition of study we find 'information' defined as 'knowledge communicated concerning some particular fact, subject, or event'.

Now we don't intend to get bogged down with definitions and we will sometimes use the words 'knowledge' and 'information' interchangeably, but for us, as the above definitions imply, information refers to knowledge which is rather specific, the kind of knowledge that might win you a prize in a quiz game. Knowledge, on the other hand, implies a depth and breadth of learning which goes beyond straightforward facts. Finding out who is the current president of the United States of America is a simple matter of information gathering, whereas gaining a knowledge of the American political system will take several years of study.

Another word we might pick up on here is 'understanding'. That is a hard word to define but we would reserve that term for the situation in which something becomes a part of the way in which you see the world. In particular it refers to the grasp of theoretical ideas and concepts rather than factual information or knowledge.

15

Well, certainly in order to obtain your degree, you have to acquire some knowledge and/or information about various aspects of society and you will find that there are many other sources besides books, as we discuss later. In this book though, we shall focus on the *process* of acquiring information or knowledge. This involves a number of skills which will not only help you to complete your degree successfully but will also be invaluable to you in later life in whatever career you decide to pursue and also in other areas of your life.

TOP TIP

Having the skill to be able to acquire knowledge is more important than the knowledge itself.

Thinking about research

Both we and our students speak of doing research for an essay and pieces of academic research may be reported as 'a study of' or 'an investigation into'. So what about this word 'research'. How does that differ from 'study'?

We all do research of one sort or another every day of our lives although we don't always call it that. How did you decide which university courses to apply to or which offers to accept? What kinds of things were important to you? Perhaps you had a particular career in mind or perhaps the discipline itself was the main attraction? Perhaps the quality of the sports facilities was the most important thing on your mind or maybe you wanted somewhere on a good train route to the town where your boyfriend is studying? Was it important to you to be in a big city with a lively night life or were you looking for somewhere with a leafy campus and plenty of green, open space? Did your choice depend on the level of fees charged?

These kinds of considerations will have produced some questions (although they may well have been implicit). Depending on what was important to you, you might have had in mind questions such as the following:

- How many students from this course go on to successful careers?
- How easy is it to get to X by train?
- What are the nightclubs like in Y?
- Does Z have a good football team?
- How much are the fees (and how much can I, or my parents, afford)?
- How good is the department of criminology?

To attempt to find the answers to these sorts of questions involves some kind of research – you probably had to read things, maybe printed brochures or websites; you may have been able to talk to people, such as previous students, admissions tutors, and so on.

Some of the answers to the above are fairly easy to find and are simply a matter of factual information:

● Is there a train service from X to Y?
● How much are the fees for studying Politics at Y?

Other questions, such as 'How good is the department?', are much more complicated. Below we look at the difficult issue of asking the right questions.

Back to our dictionary again we find that 'research' is defined as 'the systematic investigation into and study of materials, sources, etc., in order to establish facts and reach new conclusions'. And if we look up the entry for 'investigate' we are told that it means to 'inquire into; examine; study carefully' (*Concise Oxford Dictionary*, 8th edition, 1990).

So we can see that there is a lot of overlap between the words 'study', 'research' and 'investigate'. They all have something to do with 'finding out' something or acquiring knowledge but they each have slightly different connotations. The definition of 'study' that we looked at above implied that we would be mainly devoting our time to reading books and similar sources – in other words finding out information that someone else has already collected together. Although it doesn't come across in the above definition, the term 'research', certainly in an academic context, often refers to finding out things that are not already available in some form, and we will look later in this book at some of the main methods of research in this sense. 'Investigate' and 'investigation' are words that sound more at home in a murder mystery and as we shall see the 'student of society' needs to be a bit of a detective!

A major difference between the 'studying' and the 'research' that we do in our day-to-day lives and that which is required of us as students and academics is hinted at in the word 'systematic' in one of the above definitions. If our study and research as students and academics is to be effective it must be carried out in a planned and orderly fashion; and if we are to convince others of the value of our research, it must conform to certain 'rules of evidence' (more detective connotations) to which we return later.

Asking questions

The most difficult hurdle to overcome in doing research is not in learning the techniques or doing the actual work or even writing the report. The biggest obstacle, surprisingly, lies in figuring out what you want to know.

(Kane, 1985: 5)

A crucial first step in studying society is formulating useful questions and here we look at the difficulties involved in this. You probably already have quite a bit of experience of writing essays in answer to a particular question and before you gain your degree you will have a lot more! Here we will look at the kinds of questions that you may be asked to write essays on and we discuss how to think about them in ways that are useful in looking for suitable material.

As a student you may also be asked to come up with your own question for a piece of assessment. Our second-year students are expected to carry out a small piece of research on a topic of their own choosing, which means they have to devise a question which they can investigate; similarly our third-year dissertation students have to frame their topic in such a way that they know what they are looking for when they go off to the library in search of material. Whilst this might seem the easy part, it is actually the most difficult and we cannot emphasise too much the importance of thinking hard about what questions you want to ask before you begin to look for answers. Look at the following box.

Consider these questions and possible answers:

Q: Do you have the time please?
A: The time to do what?
Q: No, I mean can you tell me what the time is please?
A: Yes, I can!
Q: Well what time is it, then?
A: What time is what? When the film starts, the bus goes . . .?
Q: I just want to know what time it is now please?
A: What time it is where? London, Paris, New York?
Q: What time is it here, in Liverpool, at this moment please?
A: Why didn't you say so? It's nearly four o'clock.

Now that is a trivial example but it does illustrate our basic point which is that you need to frame your questions carefully if you are to get helpful answers. If you go off looking for information and do not have a question, then how will you know when you have found the information you need. If you do not frame your question correctly you are likely to end up with information which is irrelevant or incomplete.

Because the social sciences deal with issues that relate to our own lives/ societies, you will already have some knowledge of the topics you write about gleaned from television, newspapers, talking to friends, personal experiences and so on. You may not even be aware of some of this knowledge; much of what we know we just take for granted most of the time. Or you may have developed strong opinions about some of the issues and problems in our society or the world today. So a good place to begin is to sit down and work out what is your starting position; what do you already know about the topic; what do you think about the issues involved.

Whether what you 'know' is true is another matter, of course, and one which we will pursue later. Suppose you read in a newspaper that the crime rate is rising. Suppose you have no alternative information that gives you a reason to disbelieve such a claim. Indeed you might have heard about friends or relatives who have been victims of offences recently and that seems to reinforce the claim. So write down this bit of your knowledge:

- The crime rate is rising.

Now to produce some useful questions we turn this statement into a question:

- Is the crime rate rising?

To pursue that question takes us into even more questions to do with how we can measure and interpret crime rates.

The sorts of questions that students of society ask are driven by curiosity of some kind. Many will begin with one of the following words:

- who
- what
- where
- when
- why
- how

Try to apply these questions to the world around you.

We can also think about questions in terms of the kind of answer we might expect.

Some questions ask for descriptive answers:

- What will life be like as a student at the university of X?

Some questions ask about the relationships between things:

- Is there a link between years spent in education and lifetime earnings?

19

Some questions ask for an explanation:

- Why are men more likely to be convicted of a crime than women?

Earlier we used the example of someone trying to decide which university to choose. We pointed out that people choose a university for many different reasons and before you begin to ask questions you need to work out your starting position. So that is the first point we wish to make now. You must work out what is it important for you to know.

You should also be aware that questions sometimes come in clusters and are sometimes nested inside other questions.

Let us take one question from the earlier example:

- How much are the fees for studying Politics at Y?

This should not really be the first question. Someone asking this question may be concerned about how much it will cost them to take a degree course and is interested in finding out what the cost of studying at different universities will be. So the main question will be:

- How much will it cost me to study for a degree at University A, at University B, at University C and so on?

Asking about the fees will then be one of a series of subsequent questions, for the course fees are only one form of expenditure to be considered. What about the cost of accommodation and other living costs as well as travel to and from your home town?

Another question we considered earlier was:

- How good is the department of criminology?

A question such as 'how good is something' is seeking an evaluation. But in order to find an answer we need to know what our criteria are. What do we mean by 'good'? Good for what? So you first need to make a list of your possible criteria.

Here are some of the possible criteria on which we might evaluate a department of criminology:

- research
- teaching
- friendliness of staff
- quality of facilities, teaching rooms, etc.

20

Let us assume that, as a diligent student, you are interested mostly in the second criteria. This gives rise to another question. What are we to take as evidence of teaching quality?

University departments in the UK and elsewhere have been subject to various forms of assessment of their teaching quality over the years. So can you rely on the investigations of some outside 'quality assurance' body?

You might think that a high 'teaching quality' score means just that but six professors of economics from Warwick University wrote in *The Guardian* on 30 January 2001 that:

'Our full marks should place us among the country's elite. The world will think that, anyway. As for ourselves, we do believe we're very, very good (though not perfect). But our belief is not based on our QAA 'teaching quality' score, which does not remotely measure teaching quality in this or any other department.'

What do you make of their claim? Would you think differently if their department had received a lower score? Why?

Another possible measure might be the quality of the degrees that students receive at the end of their studies. Does a high proportion of first and upper second class honours students indicate a high quality of teaching? Well it might; but you have to remember to take into account the abilities of the students themselves. If a department is able to take in only the most able students, then you would expect them to achieve good results.

So don't take things at face value. We shall come back to this later.

Thinking around a topic

In Part V we will look at how to go about writing a final-year dissertation. Here, as an example of how to ask questions, we will consider how you might begin to think about a suitable topic.

We assume that you have chosen a general area that you are interested in. Suppose that you have decided you want to write something on 'unemployment' for example. Now whilst that might be OK to begin with, it is not going to get us very far. It needs to be narrowed down. A simple search in your university library catalogue might give you some ideas. When we searched the University of Liverpool library catalogue for items with titles beginning 'unemployment' we found 118 items and a few ideas on more specific areas to look into:

21

Unemployment in a specific country
Unemployment in a specific time period (e.g. the 1930s)
Unemployment in relation to a specific group (e.g. women or young people)
Unemployment and health
Unemployment and homelessness
Unemployment and crime
Unemployment and its social psychological effects
Unemployment and poverty
Unemployment and social policy
Unemployment and its causes

There are a number of general lessons we can learn from this little example about how to narrow down a topic to something which is manageable. One is to be specific about the country and time period that you are interested in: so 'Unemployment in Contemporary Britain' is a big improvement on 'Unemployment' but it is still too broad. Another point is that with many topics we can focus on either the causes of something or its consequences. So 'the causes of unemployment in contemporary Britain' or 'the consequences of unemployment in contemporary Britain' are beginning to sound like the sort of topics that it would be feasible to write a dissertation about. But we would still need to decide if we wanted to narrow it still further by focusing on a particular group such as young people, people from ethnic minorities or women. The list above also indicates that another good way to narrow down a topic is to link it to another one that you might be interested in; so in the above list we find unemployment linked to crime, health, homelessness and poverty, for example.

If we were to narrow down our focus any further to, say, 'crime and unemployment among young ethnic minority women in contemporary Britain' we would probably not find enough published material to be able to write a dissertation on the topic.

Another useful strategy is to think of the opposite of your main topic: so as well as unemployment think about employment; as well as the causes of crime think about the causes of law-abiding behaviour. In a similar vein if you are interested in women and unemployment, don't forget to spend some time looking at men and unemployment. If you are looking at anything and young people, don't forget to look at older people. By deliberately seeking out points of contrast and comparison in this way you can highlight aspects of your main topic which would otherwise not be obvious.

Teaching and learning in higher education

In higher education there is much less emphasis on teaching and more emphasis on learning. In other words the student has a greater responsibility for his or her

education. You need to give some attention to how you learn and what opportunities are open to you now you are at university. Here are the main settings
in which your learning will take place.

Lectures

You will probably find yourself in some very large lecture groups of maybe
300–400 students, particularly in your first year. Typically a lecture period will
last for about 50 minutes and will consist of one of your lecturers talking about
whatever the topic is. The lecturer will probably make use of various visual aids
such as PowerPoint or OHP slides or maybe video clips. There will often be
printed handouts which you may need to refer to during the lecture or they may
contain material for you to read afterwards. Listening is the most important thing
for you to do in a lecture. You will also have to take notes of course and that
is a skill which will require some work if you are to do it effectively. Here are
some key points to bear in mind:

- Put the date, title of the lecture and name of the lecturer at the top of
  the page.
- You can't write everything down so don't try.
- Concentrate on picking out the main points.
- Make a note of anything you don't understand or anything else you need
  to ask the lecturer about later.
- Within 24 hours write up your notes in such a way that they will still
  make sense to you in six months' time.
- Ask the lecturer if they can make copies of their PowerPoint or OHP
  slides available before the lecture so that you can use them to structure
  your note taking.
- Put the notes away carefully in your filing system (you do have a filing
  system don't you?).
- You won't be able to ask questions in a large lecture but please tell the
  lecturer if you can't hear them!

Lectures are a good way to get to know what the lecturer thinks are the main
points about the topic. A lecturer can't cover everything in one lecture and will
pick out the basics that he or she thinks you, the student, should know. So, when
it comes to assessment time, lecture material is what your lecturers will expect
you to know at the very least. Be warned!

Seminars or tutorials

The terms used vary from university to university and from department to department, but we are talking here about more informal classes containing probably

between 10 and 20 students. Essentially it is an opportunity for students to discuss a topic, so it is important that you make the most of the opportunity. Exploring a topic with your fellow students can be an interesting and fun way to learn but it is not so easy for the lecturer to control what goes on in these sessions, so the outcomes can be quite variable. Seminars/tutorials are also an opportunity to ask your lecturer to clarify anything you didn't understand in the lecture or in your reading. Here are some tips on how to get the most out of seminars/tutorials:

- Prepare beforehand. Your lecturer may give you a list of things to read but if not make sure you at least review your lecture notes and read any handouts.
- Join in the discussion.
- Encourage and help others to join in the discussion.

Seminars/tutorials are excellent opportunities to develop your oral communication skills and explore a topic or issue in more detail. You have not really mastered a topic until you can talk about it.

Essays

You will write a great many essays during your time at university. Essays are widely used for assessment purposes but they are also an important part of your learning. Writing an essay requires all the skills that we cover in this book – locating and searching sources of information, using them effectively, assessing them, thinking about them and communicating your thoughts in writing to your lecturers. You will find more about writing essays in Part V.

Reading

A different method of learning again is by reading books, articles, reports and so on. You have probably been reading since you were very young but reading in an academic context is a different matter to reading novels and again is a skill that you will need to work on.

Thinking about thinking

Thinking itself is a skill and one which you should focus on developing. Later we will look at some examples of how sociologists think about society. But you need to think more generally about what is involved in thinking in a structured and disciplined way. Thinking and writing are interconnected. When you write you are putting your thoughts down on paper. In doing that you make your thoughts more visible and open to scrutiny. Get into the habit of critically scrutinising your own thinking. Here are some basic building blocks of thinking.

Assumptions

These are things that we take for granted, things that we assume to be true, things that we don't examine too carefully, things for which we don't ask for proof.

Propositions

These are statements or assertions about something which can be either true or false. Evidence is needed to either prove or disprove propositions.

Arguments

We are not talking about rows here! An argument is a sequence of statements that are linked together. An argument does not depend on truth but on reason and can be either valid or invalid.

The following is an argument:

- All men like football.
- John is a man.
- John likes football.

That is a perfectly valid argument. The conclusion (John likes football.) follows *logically* from the first two statements: if they are true then the conclusion MUST be true. Conclusions of arguments such as this often begin with 'therefore', which could be defined as 'it follows that'.

The problem in this argument of course lies with the first statement – an assumption that can never be shown to be true. We can never ask all men who are living, have ever lived or ever will live if they like football. (But we could show it to be false as soon as we find one man who does not like football.) The statement 'John is a man.' is also a proposition that we could check out; 'he' could after all be a woman dressed as a man!

Practice makes perfect (well nearly – none of us is perfect!)

If you are a footballer or a musician it is easy to be aware of the skills necessary to play the game or the instrument well and you will have spent long hours practising to get it right. When you are sitting in a lecture, trying to find material in the library, reading books or writing essays, it is not so easy to appreciate that these activities also involve skills which you can develop with practice. Try to

25

become aware of your skills and to recognise when you need to practise to improve them. In the remaining sections of this book we discuss what essential skills are involved in finding out about society, understanding your sources and communicating your ideas to other people.

Part II

Finding out about society

INTRODUCTION

As we saw in Part I, we need to spend some time formulating our questions before we can begin to look for answers. It is possible that the answers to our questions can be found in some existing source – a book, a report or whatever. In this part we look at some of the possibilities and what they can offer, and in Part III we give some hints on how to use those sources effectively.

As a first example we will go back to the one we introduced earlier – choosing which university to apply for. Let us look at this from the perspective of a departmental admissions tutor. We can assume that the admissions tutor will be keen to increase applications or at least to make sure that they do not fall, in order to increase or maintain the department's intake of students. In thinking about producing publicity material in order to encourage applications he or she may well think it useful to have some information about existing applications and intakes. Some of this information is likely to be readily available – it will be routinely produced as part of the university's admission process: for example, the total number of applications, the gender distribution, the number of international students and the number of students coming via non-traditional routes. But our admissions tutor may also think it useful to know what attracted the students who eventually entered our first year and, perhaps more importantly, what influenced prospective students to choose to go elsewhere or to not even apply to us in the first place. Unfortunately the answers to these kinds of questions aren't already available and we will have to devise some ways to find out. In Part IV we discuss questionnaires, interviews, observation and other methods of research that we use to find answers to questions that no one else has found before.

Whether we are looking for information about why students choose a particular university or whether we are looking for information to help us to choose one, we are looking for answers that are truthful, correct and reliable – ones that we can use to guide our own actions. At the moment one of us is faced with the problem of three versions of a timetable for the same bus route, one at the bus stop, one on the Internet and one in a printed form from the information office. Now, in order to get home without too much trouble, it is obviously quite important to find out which of the three timetables is closest to the one used by the bus drivers. So for now, although we recognise that the question of truth is one that has exercised the minds of scholars down the centuries, we are simply going to say that what we want are truthful answers and we will look at some of the grounds which might give us confidence that an answer is truthful or that one answer is more likely to be true than another.

In Part III we will look at some of the things to bear in mind when assessing the quality of the sources available to you. In this part we look at what is on offer.

Chapter 3

Academic books and articles

As a student of society you can expect to spend a lot of your time reading books. Despite the rise of the Internet over the past 10 years or so, the printed page still seems to have a lot of life left in it. You are likely to encounter several different types of books during your time as a student. In this part we are concentrating on books and articles written by academics primarily for an academic audience – that is students and/or fellow academics. Time to get the dictionary out again! The *Oxford English Dictionary* (OED) defines an 'academic' as a 'teacher or scholar in a university or institute of higher education', which is pretty much who we have in mind, although we would not want to claim that only those who fit this description are able to produce scholarly work.

According to the OED one of the definitions of 'academic', when used as an adjective, is 'abstract; theoretical; not of practical relevance'. So you may have heard something being dismissed as 'merely' or 'only' academic. Now this suggests to us another aspect of academic study – that it is undertaken for its own sake not because it will have any practical, financial or other consequence. When someone tells us something in person, or in some other way such as in a book, one of the first questions we should ask is why are they telling us this; do they benefit in some way if we believe them. When an advertisement tells us that we will look younger if we use a certain skin product, we know that claim is being made in order to make money for the cosmetics company (although that doesn't stop even academics falling for it). Away from advertisements the benefits to those who tell us things may not be so obvious but they may be there nonetheless. If we cannot see that a person benefits from telling us a particular thing we may be more likely to believe that it is true. So our ideal type (see box overleaf) academic is someone who is selflessly pursuing truth without expecting anything in return (except the satisfaction, we hope, of finding it).

Well, reality is not quite so simple of course but at least it gives us somewhere to begin in assessing 'truth claims'. Who would you believe – the skin care commercial or the professor of dermatology?

WHAT IS AN IDEAL TYPE?

This is a term coined by one of the 'founding fathers' of sociology, Max Weber. 'Ideal' does not mean 'best' as we use it in everyday speech but refers to the typical or essential features of some aspect of social life.

'An ideal type is an abstract description constructed by accentuating certain features of real cases so as to pinpoint their most essential characteristics'

(Giddens 1997: 287)

Nevertheless, academics have careers to pursue and publishers of academic books still have to make money, so we can expect these factors to have an influence on which books are written in the first place and then which books are accepted by the publishers.

It used to be an important role of the academic presses to publish significant books too specialized to be economical to publish. Increasingly, however, as subsidies from their universities have shrunk, university presses seek to publish books they believe will make money. This too is discouraging, to put it mildly, to the investment of effort in difficult problems. Better, from the point of view of making oneself heard, to write the kind of book that might interest a trade publisher, or at least the kind of book that will get reviewed in the non-academic press. And this too, inevitably, favours the simple, startling idea, even, or perhaps especially, the startlingly false or impressively obscure idea.

(Haack, 1997)

So what will we find when we go looking for academic books?

Textbooks

First you are likely to encounter **textbooks**. These are, of course, written especially for teaching and learning purposes; they may cover a whole *discipline*, such as politics or sociology, or they may only deal with a particular specialism within that discipline, such as the sociology of the family or voting behaviour. Some may be written by one or two authors, others may be edited collections with chapters written by different authors. It is worth buying an up-to-date textbook covering the discipline you are studying at the beginning of your studies – your tutors will be able to give you advice on the best ones to consider. Such books should give you an overview of the discipline or sub-discipline and will introduce you to the main topics and ideas. Many textbooks are written to fit in with school syllabi but will also be suitable for first year university use. You should

30

be aware though, that university departments do not teach to a set syllabus in the way that schools do, so you may not find a close correspondence between your course and any single textbook. At university a textbook should only be the start of your studies and you will need to delve into the topics in much more detail, particularly after your first year. Follow up some of the suggestions for further reading or move on to a textbook that relates to a more specific topic within the discipline and follow up the references to other books and articles that you will find there.

Dictionaries, handbooks and encyclopaedias

We mentioned the usefulness of a good English-language **dictionary** in Part I. The social sciences, like the natural sciences, have developed their own 'languages' to a certain extent. Their particular approach to the world means that they may devise new words or use familiar words in perhaps unfamiliar ways. This is a characteristic of any distinctive social group with shared experiences and culture. So you will find that there are dictionaries of sociology, criminology, politics, geography, media studies, psychology and so on. These are usually geared towards the needs of students and provide a handy A–Z guide to some of the main concepts and topics of the particular discipline concerned. A language dictionary will usually only be concerned to give a concise definition of the word but these specialist dictionaries typically contain short summaries of the topic, concept or theory.

In most fields you will find there are books called **handbooks**. These are not like the instruction manuals that come with new cars or other mechanical devices; they usually seek to provide a 'state-of-the-art' guide to the subject area in the form of chapters written by specialists in different aspects of the discipline or topic. They are not only, or even mainly, directed at undergraduate students but also at other scholars and researchers, although undergraduates will usually find them of value.

You are probably already familiar with **encyclopaedias**. Well there exist specialist encyclopaedias that focus on the social sciences or on particular disciplines. One example is the *International Encyclopedia of the Social and Behavioral Sciences* (Smelser and Baltes, 2001). With 17,500 pages in 26 volumes and costing $9,995.00 in 2004, you certainly won't want to go and buy it, but you may find it in the library and it may be available to you over the Internet.

Monographs

Another important type of book that you will encounter is the one that reports on a particular piece of research or which deals with a particular issue. You will probably realise that many of the staff who teach you on your course are engaged in their own research: they are also 'studying society' in one way or another.

University lecturers are expected to pursue research and scholarly work as a part of their job and sometimes this will lead to the publication of a book. Many lecturers will have been postgraduate students and will have gained a doctorate (PhD) which is a degree awarded for the successful completion of a long thesis (typically 80,000–100,000 words). Often a lecturer's first book publication will be a version of their PhD thesis. Academic books go through a 'quality control process' in which other academics (or 'peers' – get out your dictionary again) comment on whether or not the work is worthy of publication. But academic book publishers are also commercial organisations, so that the market for a particular book can be one consideration in whether or not it is publishable. Publishers tend to specialise in publishing books in particular disciplines or collections of disciplines such as the Arts or the Social Sciences.

N.B. Don't assume that if your lecturers have published books that they are very rich – a study of crofting in the Outer Hebrides is not going to bring its author anything like the same return that the latest Harry Potter will. Your lecturers write books for a number of reasons – none of them to do with money! They write books:

- because they are expected to as a part of their job
- because it will help to further their career
- because they find their studies interesting and want to share them with others

'Learned' journals

Your lecturers will also try to get the results of their studies published as articles in 'learned' journals. Every academic discipline has its own 'learned' journals. These may cover a broad area such as the *British Journal of Criminology* or the *Sociological Review* or they may focus on a more specialised field such as *Sociology of Health and Illness* or *Marketing*. Such journals are usually published three or four times a year and contain several articles of around 8,000 words long on topics likely to be of interest to the readers of the journal. Most of these journals are published by commercial organisations, although the inclusion of a particular article will not depend on its commercial merits: instead the content of the journal will be determined by the editors of the journal These, like the authors of the articles, will also be academics such as your own lecturers. Journals have been published in paper format but now many are also available on-line: check your library catalogue for instructions on how to access them. A few journals such as *Sociological Research On-line* are only available on the Internet.

'Learned' journals also include reviews of books likely to be of interest to their readers. These can be very useful to you in providing summaries and critiques of books which may be helpful in your studies.

TOP TIP

You should make sure you find out which are the main journals covering your areas of study and look at them regularly, as they are published, to see if there are any articles that will help you with your assignments.

Journal articles are submitted to the journal editors by the authors usually after they have discussed them with other lecturers and researchers working in the same field. The editor or editors then send the article out to (typically) two or three other academics with expertise in the field to which the article relates. This is the process known as 'peer review' (did you look up 'peer'?) and it is done anonymously – the reviewers do not know the name of the authors and the authors do not know who reviews their article. The reviewer's job is to make sure that the research and scholarship on which the article is based are of high quality and that the article is making a contribution to our knowledge and is therefore worthy of publication. They may recommend that the editors accept or reject an article or they may recommend that the authors carry out certain revisions before it is acceptable. So this is basically a measure of quality control. As Roberts (1999) puts it, it is:

'one of the best tests of scholarly credibility in the academic world' and 'an important mechanism for allowing readers to make meaningful distinctions between reputable scholarly work and second-rate material'.

All of this can take some time of course. Once a draft of an article is produced it may be read by colleagues or presented at conferences, so it may be a year or so before it is polished up and submitted to a journal. One or more of the editors will read the article and decide if it is worth serious consideration. If they decide it is, then the article is sent out anonymously to the reviewers. Reviewers will have other commitments and may not be able to read the manuscript, or it may be some time before they can get around to it. So another six months or so may pass before the editors are in a position to make a decision. Depending on the

33

comments and criticisms of the reviewers, the article may be accepted as it stands (fairly unusual), rejected outright or returned to the author with suggestions for improvement. Depending on the amount of work this requires and the author's other commitments we could be talking about another six months or so before a revised version of the article is sent off to the editors. The referees are again asked to look at the manuscript to see if it has been improved satisfactorily. If it has, then the article has to join the queue to wait to be printed and published. Depending on the number of other articles in the queue and the stage of the publication cycle, it may be another year or so before the journal issue containing the article arrives in the library.

Academic writers may get little in the way of money from publishing in books but they are paid nothing at all for their journal articles. Reviewers and editors are not paid either: it is simply something that they will get involved in as a part of their job.

So an article in a peer-reviewed journal is like a car that comes with an AA or RAC warranty – it has a guarantee of quality and reliability. On the whole then, if something is written by an academic researcher we would give it a high credibility rating.

BUT that may not always be the case.

Until his death in 1971, the British educational psychologist Sir Cyril Burt was viewed as one of the most significant and influential educational psychologists of his time. Within a year of his death, however, the legitimacy of his research was being questioned. These questions began to turn into accusations, and by 1976 he was officially accused of fabricating data to prove that intelligence was inherited.

(Plucker, 2003)

Even that is not the end of the matter, however, as Plucker continues: 'The recent work of two independent researchers, Robert Joynson and Ronald Fletcher, has reopened the issue and raised doubts about the accusations of fraud'. There are usually two sides to a story and as in this case we can only read all the evidence and make up our own minds.

In 2003 a book was published by the Joseph Henry Press called *The Man Who Would Be Queen: The Science of Gender-Bending and Transsexualism*. It was written by Professor J. Michael Bailey, a psychologist and Chair of the Psychology Department at Northwestern University in the United States. It has caused some controversy, with Professor Bailey being accused of violating ethical standards of research and misrepresenting his findings. We will not rehearse the arguments here: our main point is that books coming from an apparently impeccable academic source are not necessarily above question.

Readers interested in finding more out about this controversy can find the case against Professor Bailey at these websites:

- http://www.tsroadmap.com/info/man-who-would-be-queen.html
- http://ai.eecs.umich.edu/people/conway/TS/LynnsReviewOfBaileysBook.html

And at this website you can find Professor Bailey's response to his critics:

- http://www.psych.northwestern.edu/psych/people/faculty/bailey/controversy.htm

Chapter 4

Official statistics and reports

Many of the concerns of governments are also of interest to students of society. Think about such things as education, employment, crime, health, housing, transport. Much statistical and other information about these and many other topics is assembled by various government departments either on a regular or on an occasional basis as a part of their activities.

Many social scientists have made use of government statistics in their research. One of the earliest of these was Emile Durkheim who used statistics on suicide in his famous study. Many other social scientists have treated statistical patterns and trends as 'social facts' on which to build or test their theories. Government reports can of course be useful for historical research but here we will be mainly concerned with reports on contemporary issues.

Now before you make use of official statistics you need to think carefully about them. If you want to know how many divorces were granted in the United Kingdom you can go to the UK Statistics Online website and find out that there were 166,700 in 2003 (the last year for which figures were available). Now that is a fairly concrete piece of information: whilst we can't rule out the possibility that someone may have made a mistake in counting somewhere along the line, we are not aware of any serious misgivings concerning this figure. When we look at issues such as unemployment, crime or health, however, we find that there is more room for debate about how they may be measured. Also, because they may be taken as measures of the effectiveness of government policy or of the competence of some government department, they are more open to question.

You will find that government departments and a number of 'official' bodies with a worldwide remit such as the World Health Organization also commission research and publish reports from time to time. It is often a good idea to check whether these more independent bodies come up with the same figures as government reports.

According to a report in *The Guardian*, 'Official figures showing sharp increases in gases responsible for climate change from air and freight transport were removed from the Office of National Statistics (ONS) report on the environment last week after pressure from the Department for Transport.'

> (*Officials try to hide rise in transport pollution,*
> Paul Brown, Thursday 27 May, 2004: *The Guardian*)

SOCIAL TRENDS

In the UK the Office of National Statistics has, since 1970, produced an annual publication called *Social Trends*. This publication, which you should find in your library, is also available online and 'draws together social and economic data from a wide range of government departments and other organisations to provide a comprehensive guide to British society'.

> (Office of National Statistics, 2005)

This is a valuable source of some basic information about British society on such topics as population, crime and criminal justice, education, transport, environment, housing, income and wealth, health and many more.

There are a number of questions which you should ask therefore about any official statistics:

- How have they been collected?
- Is it likely that the method of collection has influenced the results?
- Are there any other sources of similar data with which the official figures can be compared?

Other sources of statistics and reports

Of course governments are not the only bodies that produce information of interest to those of us who are studying society. In many areas, there are charitable and pressure group organisations that produce reports and other types of information relating to their field of interest. This is particularly the case with those issues that are regarded as social problems such as crime, homelessness, poverty, threats to the environment. Such organisations often make available, or highlight, information which governments or other official bodies may not wish to promote. We return to such organisations in the chapter on the Internet.

Chapter 5

The mass media

The phrase 'the mass media' or, often, simply 'the media' is shorthand for 'the media of mass communication', that is those technologies and associated organisations and professions that make it possible to communicate with large numbers of people (the 'masses'). The mass media are usually traced back to the invention, in the 1450s, of a mechanical method of printing by Johann Gutenberg, a German from Mainz. Prior to that time each book would have to be laboriously copied by hand and only a small number of educated people would have been able to access and read them. Gutenberg's invention made the mass production of books possible and set in train a revolution that would radically alter the nature of the world (Man, 2003). The development of printing and the later development of mass literacy have led to the host of books, newspapers, comics, magazines and other print media that surrounds us today.

Other new technologies have given us the photograph, the moving picture, recorded sound, radio, television and the Internet.

We are mainly concerned here with the media as potential sources of information, but clearly the media do more than just provide information: they also seek to entertain their readership or their audience. But it is not always possible to distinguish these two functions: information can be provided in an interesting and entertaining way and some entertainment can be quite informative. Nor is the line between fiction and non-fiction always easy to draw: as we write this, the BBC has screened a drama based on the case of a woman who was wrongly convicted of killing her two babies which was followed the next evening by a documentary on the same case.

Earlier we discussed the idea that academic authors produce books and articles in a selfless quest for knowledge. Whilst that might be an ideal, it does not always accord with reality, as we have seen. When we turn to the mass media, the need to attract a large audience or readership has to be the main consideration. In other words the media are concerned with making money rather than finding truth. Again this is an oversimplification. There are newspaper and television journalists who are committed to producing articles and programmes which are not necessarily popular but which attempt to address contemporary topics of concern in a serious manner (Pilger, 2004).

As with other sources of information your basic approach should be one of scepticism.

TOP TIP

We can only stress that whatever source you are using, think about who wrote it, what authority they have for saying what they say, why did they write it and who was the intended audience. Then you will be able to make a considered decision about the status of any material contained in it. In particular you should bear in mind that the media by their very nature generally focus on aspects of a topic that are of interest to a general reader or listener and that usually means those aspects that are unusual or particularly striking for some reason and these are likely therefore to be atypical.

Newspapers

Newspapers may appear on a daily or weekly basis and may be produced for a national or a local audience. National newspapers are often classified on the basis of the extent to which they are said to be 'serious', that is the degree to which they give space to political, economic and social issues compared to reports on celebrities and sport. Newspapers are also often classified on the basis of their support for various political parties and policies. And from an advertiser's point of view they can be classified according to the spending power and preferences of their readership.

The frequency with which newspapers are published means that they can report events and comment on current issues very quickly. As we saw above it can take between one and three years before an article is published in an academic journal. Clearly, newspaper journalists who have to produce reports and articles on a daily or weekly basis are not able to adhere to the conventions of academic writing, nor are they expected to. That is not to dismiss their work; some journalists write articles and books that deserve to be taken every bit as seriously as many academic tomes. Indeed the lack of a need to write in an academic format can often result in work which is more interesting and which may have a greater impact on the reader.

Some newspaper stories may be based on material published in a different format elsewhere. The publication of government reports or routine statistics will often be accompanied by press releases which summarise the material for the convenience of journalists. Obviously this may sometimes be an attempt to paint the report or statistics in a certain light. Sometimes journalists will simply base their reports on the press release; at other times, they may construct their own summary and interpretation.

Some newspaper stories, particularly in the 'serious' press, may give accounts of research published in academic journals, especially if that research is likely to be of widespread interest, links in to some issue of current concern, is unusual or is otherwise deemed 'newsworthy'.

What about the validity of newspaper reports and articles? Let us look at two headlines from the UK's *Guardian* for 24 February 2005.

'Chelsea stunned by Eto'o strike' is the headline to a report on a football match in which Chelsea were beaten by Barcelona by two goals to one. Presumably the result is a correct one and we could easily check it in most other papers, a number of websites and by a phone call to the Football Association if necessary.

The account of the match is more open to interpretation and debate, however, as will be obvious to anyone who has ever listened to a group of football supporters arguing after a match. The result still allows for differences of opinion as to which team played the best football. And in this example it would be interesting to see how the match was reported in Spain.

'Outcry at Kelly exam reforms' concerns the publication by the UK's current education secretary, Ruth Kelly, of a White Paper on the reform of the secondary school examination system. Now we have no reason to doubt that the White Paper was actually published and the brief summary of its main points could well be an accurate representation which, if necessary, we could check against the document itself. But to describe the reaction to the White Paper as an, 'outcry' is much more contentious. What actually constitutes an 'outcry'?

Newspapers are very good sources of information about the occurrence of current events. They are comparatively cheap to buy and, unlike television or radio broadcasts, they exist in a printed format which you can read and read again and which can be relatively easily stored; but reporting can be biased and newspaper articles need to be read with a healthy dose of scepticism.

40

EXERCISE 5.1

You are probably already aware of some of the main ways in which national daily newspapers differ. But to make these clear carry out the following exercise:

On one day buy as many different national newspapers as you can. Make a list of the main areas of content, for example sport, news, features and the main topics or stories in each area. Note roughly how much space is devoted to each, where in the paper the story is placed, the style of writing, the presence and type of photographs and anything else that strikes you. Make a list of the main variations that you find.

All students of society should read a quality newspaper regularly. Reports of individual events or stories about individual people can be used to good effect in essays and seminar discussions as examples of issues and topics discussed in more academic books and articles. The former are not a substitute for the latter however. Newspapers can also alert you to material which is published in full elsewhere, perhaps in a government report or an academic journal. If that material is important for the topic that you are researching, then you should go to the original source; but if it is only of peripheral interest, then you could simply refer to the newspaper report.

A recent report in the UK *Guardian* newspaper under the headline 'Lives blighted by adversity and governed by the gun' began:

> They are young men living in the shadow of the gun: deriving all their power, reassurance, self worth and respect from the very act of carrying illegal firearms. Recent research suggests that the proliferation of illegal weapons in some of Britain's most deprived communities – particularly replica and converted ones – is now such that there is a gun or an imitation firearm easily available for almost everyone who wants one.
>
> (*The Guardian*, 4 March 2005: 7)

If we follow the link to the page of the university unit that carried out the research (http://www.port.ac.uk/departments/academic/icjs/news/title, 28000,en.html) we learn that in the report the researchers 'argue that the concept of a "gun culture", often referred to in the media and by politicians, is a myth'. Yet *The Guardian* phrases 'governed by the gun' and 'in the shadow of the gun' certainly sound to us close to the idea of a 'gun culture'.

One issue of course is the length of newspaper reports compared to academic articles, reports and books. *The Guardian* article we have just referred to is just

41

over a thousand words long; the original report is 153 pages. Thus many of the qualifications and subtleties which academics are able to introduce into their arguments have to be glossed over by journalists who have a limited amount of space. Journalists are also working to tight deadlines to enable the newspaper to be on sale at the required time.

Magazines

We are not going to agonise here over the definition of a magazine. The chances are that you are, or have been, a regular reader of a magazine or two whether you are interested in style and fashion, music, motor cars, computers or any of the many other topics that you can see represented on the shelves of any large newsagent. The website of the UK store WH Smith lists over 350 titles and they are only the most popular ones. Other magazines may only be available on subscription or to members of a particular society or occupation. Typically magazines are published weekly or monthly, printed in a more permanent format than newspapers and are more concerned with ongoing topics and less with immediate news. Entertainment is likely to be the main objective, but as we noted above, the line between education and entertainment is not always clear-cut: if you are interested in horse riding, you are likely to find a magazine devoted to that topic both entertaining and educational.

Most of the mass circulation magazines are not likely to be of general interest to the student of society, although if you were carrying out research into a particular occupation such as the police, or a hobby such as ballroom dancing, you would probably find it very useful to look at some magazines directed at those topics, for example the *Police Review* (http://www.policereview.com/) or *Dance Today!* (http://www.dancing-times.co.uk/). Some magazines are, however, devoted to serious coverage of some of the topics that students of society are often concerned with, such as poverty, inequality, environmental issues and so on. Some titles that come to mind are *Time Magazine* (http://www.time.com/time/), *New Statesman* (http://www.newstatesman.co.uk/), and *New Internationalist* (http://www.newint.org/), although there are others.

Television, radio and film

In 2002, 99 per cent of UK households had access to a television set (Great Britain Central Statistical Office, 2004) and the General Household Survey of 2002 found that in the four weeks prior to the survey the most popular activity was watching television, followed by listening to the radio (Great Britain Central Statistical Office, 2004). Visiting the cinema is not such a popular activity, although in 2001, 50 per cent of young people aged 15–24 reported attending the cinema once a month or more, compared with 15 per cent of those aged 35 and over (Great Britain Central Statistical Office 2003).

There are many radio and television programmes that are educational and informative. Films made for the cinema are now primarily made with entertainment in mind, although bear in mind the point we made above that entertainment and education can coexist and some directors choose to deal with serious issues albeit in a fictional format.

> But beware – some serious issues have been given 'the Hollywood treatment' and, although they claim to represent actual events, their portrayal is actually far from the truth. The recent film 'Black Hawk Down' (Sony Pictures 2001) which purports to tell the story of the US intervention in Somalia is one such film. Check out the website http://slate.msn.com/?id=2060941 for a rundown on the '. . . fog of appealing half-truths . . .' which the website authors claim characterise this film.

One major problem with audio-visual material from a researcher's point of view is finding relevant items in the first place; you simply cannot turn up a list of television and radio programmes or cinema films in the same way that you can produce a list of books or articles. A second major problem is that, having located the details of a likely item, it may be impossible to obtain a copy of it. Major feature films are not such a problem in this respect but many television and radio programmes that were broadcast 'live' were never recorded and are lost forever. With the advent of the audio-cassette in the early 1970s followed by the video-cassette and the DVD, commercial concerns have made more material available. (See Chapter 7 for some sources of information about film and television archives.)

What about current television and radio programmes?

It is quite likely that whilst you are looking for information on a particular topic, you will come across a relevant radio or television programme that is being broadcast. After all, many of the topics of interest to students of society are also of interest to other members of that society, particularly topics that address current issues or concerns. So, if you have access to an audio- or video-recorder, you should certainly use it to record relevant programmes. But are such programmes of any use to the student of society?

Well, hearing and seeing 'real' people can certainly make an impact on your understanding of a topic. Remember what we said in Part I about the links between public issues and personal troubles discussed by Wright Mills. A television or radio documentary may well contain extracts from an interview where someone is talking about their personal experiences of being a victim of burglary or going through a divorce, for example, and may also include an 'expert' talking about the topic. But think about how the programme was constructed and why? Radio and television output will have been produced primarily to entertain: as we have said, that doesn't make it useless in educational terms but it may mean that important material – considered less entertaining – has been excluded to make sure the viewer or listener doesn't turn off. The experts and the other people appearing on the programme will be those who have responded to the programme researchers' request for help and may not necessarily be representative of those with experience of the issues or the experts in the area. Furthermore, the 'expert' contribution will have been extensively cut and many interesting points or subtleties in their point of view may be missing as a result. Such experts rarely have editorial control over the programmes in which they appear.

Nevertheless, you may well get some useful personal or other information from watching or listening to television and radio programmes which it might be difficult to obtain elsewhere. In addition, referring to a recent television or radio programme in an essay or a dissertation can show that you are tuned in to current debates, and using some of the personal stories can add a different dimension to your writing and make it more interesting. BUT you must do this carefully: you must show your reader that you are aware that material from a television programme does not carry as much weight as that from an academic article (and this applies to all media material). So use such material sparingly and preface it with phrases such as 'according to a recent television programme' or 'one example was discussed in a radio programme on . . .' which suggest that you are aware of the limitations of what you are about to discuss.

Chapter 6

Personal experience

Now as students of society, we ourselves are, of course, also a part of our subject matter. The things that sociologists and other social scientists research into and write about are all integral features of our own lives. As Peter Berger once wrote (1963: 32) 'much of the time the sociologist moves in sectors of experience that are familiar to him and to most people in his society'. When you open an introductory textbook on sociology you are likely to find, amongst others, chapters on gender relations, social stratification, and race and ethnicity. Now you probably don't use the words 'gender relations' when talking to your friends, but it would be very surprising if you weren't aware that being a boy or a girl has a big influence on your life experiences. You may never have come across the term 'social stratification' before but you can't have come this far in your life without learning that some people have more power and wealth than others and that this too has a vast influence on their lives. Nor can it have escaped your notice that our life chances and experiences may be profoundly different depending on the colour of our skin or our cultural background. Try out the following exercise:

EXERCISE 6.1

Write down your gender, your social class and your ethnicity. Then for each, write down three ways in which those attributes are likely to affect your life.

Now read the material in the boxes on pages 46–48:

MANUAL WORKERS DIE EARLIER THAN OTHERS

The health of the population improved steadily over the last century. However, there is still a strong relationship between how long people live and the nature of their jobs.

For the period 1997–99, life expectancy at birth in England and Wales for males in the professional group was 7.4 years more than that for those in the unskilled manual groups. The gap between the social classes was smaller for women than for men, at 5.7 years.

Infant mortality is a key indicator of the nation's health. The infant mortality rate fell substantially over the twentieth century in response to improved living conditions, availability of healthcare and other factors. Despite this, differentials still exist by father's socio-economic status, birthweight, marital status of parents and mother's country of birth. For babies registered by both parents, the infant mortality rate is highest for babies with fathers in semi-routine and routine occupations. Moreover, the decrease of 5 per cent in the infant mortality rate for this group between 1994 and 2002 was far smaller than the 16 per cent fall in the overall infant mortality rate.

Another indicator of health for social groups is self-reported poor health. On an age-standardised basis, reporting of poor health was highest by far among the long-term unemployed and never-worked group (19 per cent for men and 20 per cent for women) and lowest among those in the professional and managerial occupations (4 per cent and 5 per cent respectively).

Patterns of limiting long-term illness are similar to those of self-reported poor health. Among men, age-standardised rates were five times higher for those who were long-term unemployed or had never worked (43 per cent) than those in the professional and managerial group (9 per cent). The difference for women was slightly smaller, at 36 per cent and 10 per cent respectively.

(Office of National Statistics, 2004)

GENDER PAY GAP 'AS GLARING AS EVER AMONG TEENAGERS'

Lucy Ward

The entrenched split between traditionally 'male' and 'female' careers is just as glaring among today's teenagers as among their older workmates, according to new research.

A report published today finds even those entering the workplace at 16 are choosing occupations along traditional gender lines. The continuing trend means 'deep-rooted inequalities' in pay and employment prospects are mapped out for young people from the very first day of their working lives, the TUC report warns.

Even among teenagers in their first jobs, young women earn 16% less than their male counterparts – blowing apart the myth that the effect on women's careers of having children is the sole cause of pay inequality.

Union chiefs will today call on the government to challenge the stereotype images of 'jobs for the boys and for the girls', arguing that ministers should address the issue as part of wholesale reforms of 14–19 education.

The TUC says intervention is needed earlier in school careers to prevent pupils narrowing their options with choices made as young as 14.

Its report, Young at Heart? shows that 14% of young men aged 16 and 17 work in manufacturing, compared with just 6% of women of the same age. In contrast, public service jobs account for 10% of the employment of young women, and just 4% of young men.

The TUC general secretary, Brendan Barber, said: 'Until more is done to address the images of jobs for the boys and jobs for the girls, the equal pay gap will not go away.'

The finding that teenage girls earn 16% less than their male counterparts echoes recent Equal Opportunities Commission research showing female-dominated occupations generally pay lower wages than traditional 'male industries'.

Last week, the pay information body Incomes Data Services said that, far from decreasing, the gender pay gap for all workers is bigger than had been thought, standing at 19.5% for full time workers last year, and 40% for part timers, despite government insistence it was tackling the issue.

The report comes on the day of a 'gender and productivity summit' at 11 Downing Street, aimed at establishing the economic and business case for reducing sex inequality and closing the gender pay gap.

Source: *The Guardian*, Tuesday 26 October 2004
Guardian Unlimited © Guardian Newspapers Limited 2004

EXCLUSION ZONE

Older universities in particular must address their image issues if they want to attract ethnic minority students, says Tessa Blackstone – but all institutions need to do more.

There are more black and ethnic minority students in higher education than ever before: 250,000 at the last count, comprising one in eight of all home students. That is a real success story. These students have shown ambition and tenacity in getting to university.

But, despite the achievements of so many, there is still a long way to go before British universities fully represent the communities they serve. A particular challenge faces us in the case of young black men of African-Caribbean origin. As Trevor Phillips of the Commission for Racial Equality (CRE) has pointed out, more young black men enter prison each year than enter university. It is a shocking statistic that raises important issues for universities, as well as posing challenges for the penal system and our schools.

Source: *The Guardian*, Tuesday 26 October 2004
Guardian Unlimited © Guardian Newspapers Limited 2004

Make a list of the main points in these three articles. Which ones were you already aware of and which ones were new to you?

In addition to gender, social stratification and ethnicity, common topics in introductory sociology textbooks are the family, education, work, leisure, religion, the mass media – all of which you have some experience of directly or indirectly. You will also know something about some of the phenomena usually depicted as 'social problems' – crime, poverty, divorce, homelessness, problem drug use – for, even if neither you nor anyone you know has personal experience of these problems, you can hardly have escaped being aware of these aspects of the society in which you live.

Most of the time we are not aware of what we know about the world in which we live, we simply take it for granted. We don't spend large amounts of our time analysing what is going on in our lives or at least we don't when things are as we think they should be. When things are going wrong, when something becomes a problem, then we tend to think more about it. Students of society often are concerned about some of the *problems* of their society, but as Peter Berger says, they are as likely to be interested in how society works 'normally' as when it goes wrong in some way.

Now, a few comments on the use of personal experience. First, that is exactly what it is – your personal experience – no one else's. You are a unique human being and no one else will have exactly the same experiences as you. But at the same time you share certain characteristics and life events with other people: your gender, the fact that you are a student in higher education, your language, your cultural background. People around you may tell you about their own personal experiences and you can see which way these differ from your own and which way they may be similar.

Two opposite assumptions are commonly made when it comes to using information based on personal experiences. First, people sometimes assume that the way they experience or think about something must be similar to everyone who has similar characteristics to them or everyone who has been through similar experiences to themselves. So you will hear people say things like: 'I know what it is like to be . . . burgled, . . . an only child, . . . unemployed' or whatever the subject is. But each person experiences such matters in a deeply personal way. The second assumption, however, is to discount personal experience because that is all it is – one person's view. Often students are not encouraged to reflect on their own life experiences, although these are the starting point for any understanding of the world.

Neither of these assumptions is necessarily wrong or necessarily right. All we would encourage you to do is to take a sceptical approach and treat information based on personal experiences in the same way that you would treat any other kind of information. So when a person says: 'I know what it is like', what they really mean is: 'I know what it was like for me'. Whether their experience is similar to others is a matter for investigation. But we certainly shouldn't discount our own experiences or those told to us by the people we know: they are valuable sources of information, although we should remember that, for various reasons, people don't always tell the truth or tell the whole story – even to themselves! But that gets us into rather a complicated area which we won't pursue here.

Chapter 7

The Internet

In 2003, 54.6 per cent of US households had access to the Internet (US Department of Commerce, 2004). In 2004, 52 per cent of United Kingdom households had access to the Internet (Great Britain Central Statistical Office, 2005). Fifteen years ago the only students likely to make much use of computers were those studying computer science, mathematics or statistics. Today education at any level and in any subject is inconceivable without computers. Your university or college will almost certainly provide you with some training in the use of computers and the Internet: DON'T SKIP THIS. You will need IT skills to complete your course successfully and you will also find that they are highly marketable skills when it comes to pursuing your chosen career.

As Arms (2002) points out, 'a marvelous assortment of high-quality information is available on line', but he goes on to point out that there is also much 'material that is inaccurate, biased, sloppy, bigoted, wrongly attributed, blasphemous, obscene, and simply wrong'. Ó Dochartaigh (2002: 6) too writes that the Internet, 'plays host to "hate" politics, to child pornography and to the obscenities and ravings of lonely individuals with nothing better to do than vent their frustration online'.

Like any technological development, the advent of the Internet has had positive and negative consequences. On the positive side it can facilitate communication across the globe and make available vast amounts of information and expertise to anyone with access to a networked computer. On the other hand, anyone with access to the Internet can produce webpages irrespective of the quality of the content. Webpages are not 'peer reviewed'. The development of software that enables professional looking webpages to be produced with ease only compounds the problem so that it may be at first glance difficult to distinguish 'the ravings of lonely individuals' from the considered thoughts of world authorities.

We can be reasonably certain that the books and journals we find in our university library will meet the academic standards that we discussed earlier. But once we have found some relevant online material we have the additional problem of deciding if it is worth our attention. So problem two with Internet-based material

A library of books is useless unless we can find the books we need. That is why libraries have catalogues: they enable us to find a particular book by its author and by its title and they also enable us to find what books are in the library on a particular topic. The sheer quantity of material available on the Internet means that finding what we want in the way that we can find what we want in the library is immensely more complicated. So problem number one is finding relevant material; in Part III we discuss some of the ways in which you can do this.

is one of quality control. Later we will discuss how to sort out the good from the bad and the ugly online.

Journals

The first thing to point out is that some of the information available on the Internet is simply an electronic version of many other sources of information. If you log on to a networked computer and go to the catalogue of your university library you should find that many of the academic journals relevant to your discipline are available to you online – the more recent volumes that is – some academic journals are a hundred or more years old and earlier volumes are not usually available electronically.

Most students entering university straight from school in the early years of the twenty-first century will barely remember a time without the Internet, so it is worth reflecting on how new this use of computer technology is. The Internet as we know it today has only been in existence since 1993/4. The IBM personal computer only became available in 1981 and it was only in the early 1980s that we were able to exchange typewriters for word processors, thereby enabling our writings to be stored in an electronic format. So you can imagine that making material which is not in an electronic format (that is older than 1980) available on the Internet in any quantity is quite a task. (For more information on the history of computers and the Internet see http://www.computer history.org/)

So all that we said earlier about learned journals applies here too: the Internet version of a journal article can be treated in exactly the same way as its printed counterpart. It will usually be easier to locate articles on particular topics using a networked computer, as we discuss in Part III, and when you have found what you are looking for it will usually be easier to save a copy and print it out from your computer than to photocopy a paper version.

Books

It is sometimes possible to find complete books on the Internet (see http://online books.library.upenn.edu/archives.html), although this may not be as useful as it might first appear. Project Gutenberg (http://www.promo.net/pg/) is a collection of over 13,000 out-of-copyright books which can be downloaded free of charge. Because the books have to be out of copyright most of those available were originally published in the 1920s or earlier. The books are chosen by volunteers who turn the book into an electronic format, so whether there is a book available which is useful to you is not guaranteed. Many of the texts which are to be found on Project Gutenberg, such as novels by Jane Austen or Thomas Hardy, are ones which should be in any well-stocked library or which can be bought in a second-hand bookshop for probably less than the cost of downloading and printing.

However some classic texts, such as those of the early sociologists, will be available online and this can be a very useful format in which to study them. Electronic documents have search facilities so that you can type in keywords or phrases and find the full text you are looking for instantaneously – so it is worth checking if the material which you are studying is online.

Official reports and statistics

Most reports and statistics produced by national governments or international political bodies are freely available in an electronic format. The following are some that you might find particularly useful:

- The US Census Bureau (http://www.census.gov/index.html)
- The UK Home Office (http://www.homeoffice.gov.uk/rds/index.htm)
- The UK National Statistics Online (http://www.statistics.gov.uk/)
- The United Nations (http://www.un.org/)
- The World Health Organization (http://www.who.int/en/)
- The European Union (http://europa.eu.int/)

Non-governmental organisations

As we noted above, there are many non-governmental organisations working in areas that relate to many of the topics that interest students of society. The easiest way to access the information produced by such organisations is via their websites.

Below we give a few examples of the kind of organisations which we have in mind. Find out which organisations are active in the fields in which you are interested.

- Amnesty International (http://www.amnesty.org/) is an organisation that is concerned with abuses of human rights.
- Friends of the Earth (http://www.foe.co.uk/) and Greenpeace (http://www.greenpeace.org/international_en/) are two well-known organisations concerned with environmental issues.
- Global Call to Action Against Poverty (http://www.whiteband.org/) is just what is says – an international organisation working to tackle poverty.
- The Howard League for Penal Reform (http://www.howardleague.org/) and NACRO (http://www.nacro.org.uk/) are two UK organisations working in the Criminal Justice field.
- Shelter (http://england.shelter.org.uk/home/index.cfm) is a UK organisation concerned with issues of housing and homelessness.

Newspapers and magazines

Most newspapers and magazines have their own webpages. In the section on magazines above, most of the references were in fact to the websites of the publications mentioned. That is because, sitting at our computers, it is easier to look online at what is available than to walk over to the library or the nearest newsagent. Until the recent advances in information technology, searching for reports or articles on particular topics was very time consuming. Today it is much easier and you will probably find that your university library subscribes to a search facility called Lexis Nexis which will enable you to (amongst many other things) locate newspaper articles on your chosen topic. Most libraries and particularly university ones usually only subscribe to the 'serious' titles in their printed form, but with the advent of the Internet most newspapers have a website at which you can access current and past articles and reports, often without charge. There will also be links to other material which relate to the topic of the article or report. However, accessing a newspaper on the web will mean that you are unable easily to set the article in its context; that is – what else did the newspaper report on that day, where in the newspaper was the article printed and how prominent was it? You will also not know which images accompanied the text – so searching for newspaper articles online is not always the best option.

You will find that if you need to search for material which is earlier than the 1980s you will have to look through paper copies. An exception is *The Times* (London) which is available in a digital format from 1785 to 1985, if your library has access to it.

Archives

The Internet is also an excellent means of locating and sometimes viewing material which is held in archives. An archive is simply a collection of documents and records and sometimes other artefacts. Organisations of one kind or another usually archive such things as correspondence, records, files, minutes of meetings and so on for reference and legal purposes. Sometimes archives exist which are dedicated to a particular topic or even a specific person (see the boxes below). Such material can often be useful to students of society particularly those pursuing historical research.

THE CONTEMPORARY MEDICAL ARCHIVES CENTRE AT THE WELCOME TRUST

(http://library.wellcome.ac.uk/archmss.html#P10_2042)

The Contemporary Medical Archives Centre (CMAC) was founded in 1979 with the aim of collecting and preserving records illuminating 20th-century developments in medicine, biomedical science and healthcare, concentrating on material in English created in Britain or parts of the former Empire.

Besides the papers of many individuals who contributed to the field, from Nobel Prize-winning scientists to GPs and lay individuals, records of numerous professional bodies, learned societies, research institutions, charities, campaigning organizations and propagandist associations have been acquired, as well as some business archives. We now hold over 700 separate collections of archives and papers of organizations and individuals, and the number is constantly increasing. In 1989 the CMAC received a number of accessions from the Wellcome Tropical Institute, which was active between 1985 and 1989, including the Royal Army Medical Corps Muniment Collection which contains material on military medicine from the 18th to the late 20th centuries.

THE JOHN WYNDHAM ARCHIVE AT THE UNIVERSITY OF LIVERPOOL

(http://www.sfhub.ac.uk/Wyndham.htm)

The John Wyndham Archive is the author's Estate Collection. It contains a large number of holograph manuscripts and corrected typescripts of his novels and short stories (including several unpublished and incomplete works), non-fiction articles and scripts for radio, screen and stage plays. John Wyndham was a very private man and, wishing to be judged solely on his work, instructed that his personal papers be destroyed. However, the Archive does contain large quantities of letters to and from various editors and publishers, some fan mail and a collection of over 350 letters to his life-long partner Grace Wilson that reveal Wyndham's thoughts and experiences during the Second World War. There are also some taped conversations between Wyndham and his brother, Vivian Beynon Harris.

Some useful archive websites

- The National Archives (http://www.nationalarchives.gov.uk/)
- The US National Archives & Records Administration (http://www.archives.gov/)
- The UK film and television archives (http://www.movinghistory.ac.uk/archives/index.html)

Subject guides

If you have used the Internet before you will be familiar with using a keyword search engine such as Google (http://www.google.com/). Such search engines can be an effective way of finding what you are looking for if you have something very specific in mind but you don't know the URL (see box below) that will lead you to it. For example, if you know there is an organisation called the 'Child Poverty Action Group', typing that into Google will reward you with a list of over 3 million links but the first one will take you to where you want to go.

URL = uniform resource locator. This is the address of a document or file on the World Wide Web. For example http://www.liv.ac.uk/sspsw/ is the URL of the Department of Sociology, Social Policy and Social Work Studies at the University of Liverpool.

But using Google to search for material on a topic such as 'Poverty' or 'Crime' will produce a list of a large number of websites (try it and see how many!) and you are then faced with the problem of deciding which ones are going to be useful to you.

Universal subject directories such as those available at Yahoo (http://dir. yahoo.com/) can also sometimes be useful. These are a bit like an online Yellow

Pages directory but alongside the sections on entertainment or recreation you can find sections on society and culture which can sometimes yield useful sources. For serious academic work, however, it is best to use a subject directory which is concerned primarily or exclusively with academic sources.

One of the oldest universal subject directories is the **WWW Virtual Library** (http://vlib.org/). This is a collection of guides to webpages on various subject areas. The Social and Behavioural Sciences section, for example, list sites concerned with Anthropology, Archaeology, Demography, Economics, Migration and Ethnic Relations, Psychology and Sociology amongst others. Each site is maintained by different people around the world and consists of a guide to further websites relevant to the area which have been screened for quality and accuracy. The Social Policy section of the WWW Virtual Library, for example, is maintained at the University of Bath in the UK.

THE RESOURCE DISCOVERY NETWORK (RDN)

(http://www.rdn.ac.uk/)

This is the UK's free national gateway to Internet resources for the learning, teaching and research community. The service currently links to more than 100,000 resources via a series of subject-based information gateways (or hubs). The RDN is primarily aimed at Internet users in UK further and higher education but is freely available to all.

In contrast to search engines, the RDN gathers resources which are carefully selected by subject specialists in our partner institutions. You can search and browse through the resources, and be confident that your results will connect you to web sites relevant to learning, teaching and research in your subject area.

Part of the RDN is the **Virtual Training Suite** (http://www.vts.rdn.ac.uk/) which is a set of online tutorials 'designed to help students, lecturers and researchers improve their Internet information literacy and IT skills'. It is freely available and consists of a set of different tutorials focused on different subject areas.

Another invaluable Internet resource specifically concerned with the Social Sciences is the UK-based **Social Science Information Gateway** (http://www.sosig.ac.uk/) which 'is a freely available Internet service which aims to provide a trusted source of selected, high quality Internet information for students, academics, researchers and practitioners in the social sciences, business and law' (http://www.sosig.ac.uk/about_us/what_is.html). Each of the resources which you can access via SOSIG (pronounced 'sausage'!) has been selected and is described by a librarian or academic.

Part III

Using your sources

INTRODUCTION

This part is concerned with various strategies and techniques which you can employ to identify and collect specific sources of information. It looks at how to collect information in a systematic way, about how much information to collect and when to limit searches. It also looks at how to get the most out of electronic searches by using keywords and phrases and linking these with Boolean operators. We also explore ways of filing and ordering the information that you find, whether in electronic or non-electronic form, to ensure that it can be more easily retrieved and used in various projects.

PRIMARY AND SECONDARY DATA SOURCES

In this book we concentrate on collecting information from *secondary* data sources. These are sources of information which already exist. If you were to set out to collect your own data, it would be referred to as a *primary* data source as you would be the first person to have collected it.

Every researcher should collect all the information which they can from *secondary* sources of data before they set out to do their own research.

This ensures that their work is located in an existing body of literature. It is also very important that researchers do not waste both their own and the researched population's time repeating work that has already been adequately completed

In Part II we explored various sources of information and the relative merits and disadvantages of each. In this part we will look in more detail at how you can get the most out of your searches.

THE RESEARCH PROBLEM

When you are conducting research into any area, whether you have a set question to address or not, it is useful to think in terms of solving a 'research problem', i.e. what is the problem or question which your essay or piece of research is to address. Then structure your work in a way which will help to 'solve' that problem.

This will help you to devise a logical and coherent structure for your work.

Chapter 8

Search strategies

When you are looking for information to help you to answer a particular question it is very important that you develop **a search strategy**. That is that you think carefully about the sort of information that would be useful to you before you start to conduct any sort of search. Developing and refining your search strategy is probably the most difficult part of any research which you carry out. This is where you really focus on how to answer your question and which pieces of information you consider will be most useful to you.

There are a number of stages which you must go through in order to devise a successful search strategy:

DEVISING YOUR SEARCH STRATEGY

- Identify the key issues.
- Choose the relevant information sources.
- Decide on keywords for your searches.
- Construct a keyword diagram.

Stage One: Identifying the key issues

This is an extremely important part of the process. It is the base on which the rest of your strategy stands or falls. So how do you do this and how do you make sure that you have covered all aspects of your study? It takes a bit of thinking and some initial general reading around the topic.

First, do you have a set question?

Yes, there is a set question

Then use the question, and break it down into its separate parts in order to help to identify what the key pieces of information will be.

Example: Why are men more likely to commit crime than women?

This question:

1 asks questions concerning the **extent** of offending
   (a) it asserts that men commit *more* crime than women
2 is concerned with **explanations** of offending behaviour
   (a) it asks the question Why . . .?
3 asks for **comparison**
   (a) of the nature and extent of offending by sex
   (b) and is concerned with comparing explanations of the offending behaviour of men with explanations of the offending behaviour of women

So, take each of these components one by one:

1 The extent of offending

First you will have to examine the assertion that men commit more crime than women. In order to do this you will have to look at who commits most crime. If the answer is men, then is this true for all crimes or are there some crimes which women commit more often than men or equally as often?

So **statistics** on crime will be important here. These will help you to address:

- the extent of offending behaviour amongst men;
- the extent of offending behaviour amongst women;
- whether the assertion that men commit more crime than women is true;
- whether this holds true in all circumstances.

2 Explanations of offending behaviour

You will need to explore theories which seek to explain why men commit crime and theories which seek to explain why women commit crime. To explore **theories** surrounding the offending behaviour of both men and women you will have to read some theoretical literature – which is most commonly found in academic studies in books and journal articles (and sometimes the webpages of academics). You will find this literature either in the library or in some sort of electronic form – Part II of this book takes you through some relevant sources. These sources will help you to address:

- explanations of male offending behaviour;
- explanations of female offending behaviour.

3 Comparisons of offending behaviour

Lastly you will have to **compare** the theories on offending behaviour of males and those of females.

- What are the different explanations for offending behaviour?
- Are there any similarities?
- Do these different theoretical perspectives help you to answer the question set?
- How do they help?

So if you were to set out the various stages which you must go through in order to carry out the necessary research for your essay, they would look something like this:

1 Isolate the key issues – what is the question asking you to do?
2 Collect the necessary data.
3 Find and read the relevant theoretical literature.
4 Analyse the relevance of the literature to the research problem.

What if there is no set question?

If there is no set question then you will have to devise one of your own. To do this you should focus on some aspect of the subject which interests you and set your own question. Then go through the same process as outlined above.

For example, perhaps you have been asked to write a piece on women and crime. This is a huge topic and you would have to narrow it down substantially before you could begin to start to search for relevant information.

The way to focus your research when you are not set a particular question is to determine in which area of the subject you are interested and to consider the questions which that aspect of the subject throws up. You can only do this by reading around the very broad area – in this example, of women and crime – and choosing one aspect which is of interest to both yourself and the area of study around which you are writing. You do not have to read too much before you narrow your focus. Think about the lectures you have attended and the discussions which have been generated in the classroom, look at some relevant chapters in textbooks. You will soon find that there are a number of important questions surrounding the study of women and crime, one being why women appear so less frequently in criminal statistics than do men. Of course, there are many, many important areas which could be explored such as the pattern of female offending, or women as victims of crime rather than perpetrators, or women's fear of crime and so on; but for the purposes of this example we will assume that you have decided to look at why women appear to be less involved in offending than males. You now have a question which your work can set about trying to answer, i.e. why does it appear that men are more likely to commit crime than are women.

Stage Two: Choosing the relevant sources

Available information sources

Next you must consider which sources will be most appropriate for you to use in order to collect the necessary data, and to find the theoretical literature for your study. There are various places which you can go to find this information. See Part II for a more detailed discussion of the various sources of information available to you. However, remember that these include the following:

- *Your module reading list* Course tutors generally supply a reading list. This is a good place to start – reading lists will include the books, journals, etc. most appropriate for study of the subject.
- *The library* If you cannot get hold of the books on the reading list, then you will have to find alternatives. Carry out a search on your library catalogue to find which books are stocked in that area. Try looking for books which have the same classification number as those which are on the reading list.
- *Journals* Journals are a good source of research, many will specialise in the area in which you are interested and can provide quite up-to-date information on a topic as the latest volumes will report the very latest research and writing in a particular area.
- *The World Wide Web* The Internet is now the source of a vast amount of information, much of which is very useful. Part II outlines various sources which you can use and strategies for finding relevant and valid information on the Internet.
- *Government reports and statistics* Again, many of these can now be found on the Internet and can be accessed from any computer linked to the Internet, immediately you need them.

TOP TIP

Do not rely on using general Internet search engines alone. It is very easy to carry out all your searches using a search engine such as Google and you will find results this way. However, using subject-specific engines and gateways will result in the identification of sources which are more relevant for academic study.

Narrowing down your searches

You cannot read everything that is available on your chosen topic, however, so it pays to focus your search, to narrow it down to a more manageable exercise. You can do this in a number of ways:

- Use reliable, tried and trusted sources for your data. Do you need crime statistics, for example? Then consider which are the best sources of data on crime. Might this be government or police sources? Are there any other sources which routinely and regularly update crime figures? Which have you used before? Were they useful?
- Which sources would be most likely to elicit relevant information on explanations of offending behaviour. You should consider whether you are answering the question from the point of view of psychology, sociology or history – each discipline has subject-specific information sources.
- Are you looking at offending behaviour in the UK, the US, across the Middle East, or Africa? Each of these geographical regions will have its own sources and methods of collecting data. This may seem obvious but remember that if you are comparing statistics across regions you will not be comparing like with like as each country collects its statistics in different ways.
- You also need to determine which time frame you are using – will you cover the past 10 years, the past 50 or will you go back further? Remember to state in your work which time period you are focusing on and use information/writing relevant to that time period.

Example:
HOW TO CHOOSE YOUR SOURCES OF INFORMATION

In the example above we identified the key areas of the research question as:

- Statistics on crime
- Explanations of male offending behaviour
- Explanations of female offending behaviour

Further questions to focus your work:

- What time period will I cover?
  Possible answer – post-Second World War

65

- What country/countries am I interested in?
  Possible answer – England and Wales

- In which general area of study am I engaged, e.g.
  sociological/psychological/historical?
  Possible answer – Sociological

Choosing relevant sources:
- Home Office – England and Wales
- Criminal Statistics post-Second World War
- University library catalogue
- Sociology-related works
- UK-based journals
- UK-based electronic resources
- UK-based web-searches

Chapter 9

Search techniques

Keywords

Now you have:

1 Decided on your research question, or problem.
2 Identified the main issues you will need to cover.
3 Decided which sources you will use.

Your next step is to search for relevant information. You can do this randomly – but it is much better if you identify some **keywords** which can help you locate the right information as efficiently as possible. In this next section we will introduce you to the idea of the **keyword diagram.**

Every researcher uses keywords to help them find information. Keywords are used in all sorts of ways, by all sorts of institutions in order to make information easier to find and to sort. Keywords are:

- used by publishers to allocate ISBN numbers to every book and some published reports. ISBN stands for International Standard Book Number and all books published in most countries have a unique ISBN attached to them
- used by libraries to classify all their material into particular categories so that they are easier to find using their catalogues
- used by publishers of journals to ensure that articles printed in each journal issue can be more easily found
    - journals will also publish an annual index which uses keywords to help the researcher find relevant articles published that year
    - most journals now have electronic search facilities on their webpages so that researchers can browse all articles they have published, though sometimes these are limited to a few years' publications

- used by Internet search engines. Anyone who has used the Internet to search for information will have put keywords into the search box to help them find information.

So you can see that keywords are regularly used to help us catalogue (sort) and to find (research) relevant information.

It is worth giving some thought to the keywords which you use in order that you find the relevant information which you need as easily and quickly as possible.

Example 1:
LOOKING FOR INFORMATION: USING THE INTERNET

What if you wanted to find out how many people in the United States had ever used the Internet to send an email? It would make sense to look for a report on Internet use. You could look for this in the library, but as we have seen, many statistics are found on the World Wide Web. So we could easily start there. In this example we have used the Google search engine, although as we have pointed out earlier, the use of more subject-specific gateways can produce more relevant information more quickly.

What keywords would you use in your search engine?

In January 2005 we typed the terms *Internet* and *United States* into Google. We got 43,500,000 hits – this is far too many to be of any use to the researcher and many of them were not related to the use of email at all.

We then typed in *Internet* and *United States* and *email*.

Straightaway we got rid of around 18,000,000 hits, but 25,200,000 is still too many.

We could carry on by just putting more keywords into the search engine; for example *Internet* and *United States* and *email users* generated fewer hits again at 9,530,000 but this is still far too many.

It would be more efficient to think a little about what you are trying to find. Remember you are looking for statistics on email use in the United States. So instead try using keywords which describe exactly what you want. We typed in *Internet use surveys United States*.

Immediately we came across a page hosted by the University of Maryland, College Park. The page was called 'Scientific Research on the Internet' and it listed, and linked to, a number of surveys conducted in the United States by the US Census Bureau and other reputable organisations, such as Pew Internet Surveys.

One survey on the list was the 'CPS Internet and Computer Use Supplement (September 2001)'.

It was possible, by linking to this, to interrogate the actual data collected on every variable included in the survey. It included a number of interesting and relevant variables, but they were difficult to understand in their raw (unanalysed) form. We therefore tried to find out if there was a report on this data which had already been analysed.

To do this we typed 'CPS Internet and Computer Use' into our search engine. We instantly found the CPS (Current Population Survey) homepage. We followed the links:

- CPS Computer Ownership Supplement – Methodology and Documentation Page
- Computer Ownership
- 2003 Internet and Computer Use Data

and found: A Nation Online: Entering the Broadband Age. This was described as:

> The sixth report released by the U.S. Department of Commerce examining the use of computers, the Internet, and other information technology tools by the American people. Based on the U.S. Census Bureau's Current Population Survey of 57,000 households containing 134,000 persons, this report provides broad-based and statistically reliable information on the ways that information technologies in general, and broadband more specifically, are transforming the way we live, work, and learn.
>
> (U.S. Department of Commerce 2004)

We followed this link and found the following statistics presented in this report:

> The proportion of U.S. households with computers reached 61.8 percent in 2003, and 87.6 percent of those households used their computers to access the Internet.
>
> E-mail remains the most prevalent online activity, with 87.8 percent of Internet users sending and receiving e-mail or instant messaging.

BINGO! A little more focus and we found exactly what we wanted and it took less than half an hour.

So your choice of keywords is very important. You should tailor these to the particular type of information you want to find and the sort of source which you are using to find the information.

Look again at Example 1 above. What if you had chosen to look in the library to find out how many people in the United States used email?

Libraries are great sources for information which is found in book form. Although many libraries have now branched out to include videos and CDs, their main, long-standing, collections are those which present the written word. Libraries do also have collections of statistics and reports, but with the advent of the World Wide Web it is often more effective to look for reports and other sorts of non-book publications on the net, and it is cheaper to access this material on the web, where it is often freely available, rather than to buy in hard copies of the same publications. However, libraries are the only places where books can be found for free. Because of copyright laws, and the publisher's need to cover publishing costs, there are very few books which can be accessed on the web, so you will need to use library collections throughout your studies.

Example 2:
LOOKING FOR INFORMATION: USING THE LIBRARY

Remember that in Example 1 we were looking for information on how Americans use the Internet. For that search we found that the keywords *Internet use surveys United States* generated the best links. We typed these words into the search facilities of the University of Liverpool library and found ABSOLUTELY NOTHING. This is because the average library does not contain the millions of pieces of information which are found on the web, so the keywords which you choose and which work on the Internet will often not work in other information databases such as library catalogues.

When searching on the web we found there was so much information that we had to NARROW our focus, whereas the library is a much smaller repository of information so we have, instead, to BROADEN our focus. The BROADEST terms we used to find information on email use in the United States were *Internet* and *United States*. We typed this into the library's search facility instead and were rewarded with a list of 23 books which were published between 1995 and 2003.

We looked at the 23 books which the library search facility found for us. These were on quite a range of topics on the Internet, from legal issues surrounding the Internet through manuals on how to use the Internet to conduct your own research. The results of this search confirm that using the library catalogue is not the most efficient way to find specific pieces of information. Maybe none of these books contain the information we were looking for on how many people in the United States use email, and even if they did we would have to take a trip to the library, find the books on the shelves and read through them to see what they contained. This could take hours, even days, whereas the Internet search took under half an hour. And even if we did find that one of the books contained this information it might not be as up to date as the information found on the web; after all, the latest book on the list was published in 2003 and would probably have been written the previous year.

Books are most useful, therefore, for finding ideas rather than facts and for discovering theories rather than statistics, and also for showing how different ideas and perspectives have been presented and developed over time.

If we were to limit our library searches to the first keywords we found useful, we would miss out on locating some key texts. This is because the keywords chosen by the author or publisher to describe their work, or that chosen by the librarian to catalogue the collection, might be different from the ones we have chosen. Take, for example, our search on the United States and uses of the Internet. In the library search we used the keywords *Internet* and *the United States*; however, there are other words which mean the same thing and could just as easily be used as substitutes for the first words we chose. For example, we might substitute *World Wide Web* or *cyberspace* for *Internet* or *America* for *United States*.

By substituting these RELATED terms we found another 10 books.

Example 3:
LOOKING FOR INFORMATION: USING JOURNALS

We used the *ISI Web of Knowledge* to search for journal articles on Internet use in the United States. Once again this demonstrated the importance of using RELATED terms to find articles that use different keywords and NARROWER terms to make the search more manageable.

ISI Web of Knowledge searches over 5 million documents to find articles which use the same keywords which you have chosen. This means that you will find that you often have to NARROW your search to find relevant documents on such complete databases.

The following terms, although all similar, generated a very varied number of hits using the Web of Science search facility:

Keywords used	No of articles found
Internet and United States	294
Internet and America	108
Email and United States	6
Email and America	3
Cyberspace and United States	25
Cyberspace and America	9
World Wide Web and United States	42
World Wide Web and America	10

This shows the importance of continuing to search a database using RELATED terms. To use one combination of keywords alone might mean missing the majority of articles in your area of interest.

Constructing a keyword diagram

To devise a successful search strategy, then, you will have to consider:

- your initial choice of KEYWORDS
- RELATED words
- BROADENING your search
- NARROWING your search

In order to do this you should construct a **keyword diagram** which includes all the terms which you might use.

To begin constructing your keyword diagram you should first go back to your question and identify the **key issues** which you should focus on. Use these key issues to decide on the keywords which you will start with.

Sample question: How would you explain the 'digital divide'?

This question asks for an **explanation** of the phrase the 'digital divide'. Explanation can include:

- definition
- giving a clear and detailed account of something

So first you must:

1 Define the term 'digital divide'.
2 Explore whether it exists.
3 Outline clearly how it is manifested.
4 Look at theories which account for its existence.

The first keywords which you should use are clearly the term itself *digital divide*, but this will not be enough on its own. You will also need to look at RELATED, NARROWER and BROADER terms.

To find RELATED words you will first have to find a definition of what the digital divide is. How do you know what else to call this if you do not know what it is in the first place; and how else will you know how to narrow or broaden your search?

A quick search on the Internet using the keywords *digital divide* quickly reveals that the term refers to inequality in access to, and knowledge of, computer technologies such as the Internet. This divide is said to exist as clearly *within* developed countries as *between* different regions of the world.

Now that you have read something about the topic it is easier to find RELATED, NARROWER and BROADER keywords to complete your search.

You can now start to construct a **keyword diagram** similar to the one below:

	KEYWORDS	
	Digital divide	
NARROWER	RELATED	BROADER
Internet use AND Gender Race Education	Computers AND Poverty Inequality	Technology Cyberspace AND Social exclusion

Figure 9.1 *Keyword diagram*

- As you can clearly see, the RELATED keywords substitute words which *mean the same as* digital divide.
- The BROADER words go beyond computers alone and look at technology or cyberspace in general and *widen the scope* of your enquiry.
- The NARROWER terms *focus on particular aspects* of computer use and particular dimensions of exclusion.

N.B. The keyword diagram drawn above has been designed to help you understand the process involved in the construction of such a diagram. It includes basic suggestions as to how you might focus your research. Your own keyword diagram might have looked quite different – if so, it would not necessarily be 'wrong'. There are many ways in which you could focus this question – you could decide to look at the digital divide within the United States alone, or you might want to contrast computer use in Europe with that in Africa. In these cases your keyword diagram would look very different. It is a tool to help you focus your research and its design should be approached with this in mind.

EXERCISE 9.1

Keyword diagrams are not easy to construct. They take some time and thought and will involve some initial reading around the topic. They do become easier with time, so practise constructing such diagrams using the following initial keywords:

Gender and Crime
Trade Unions and Decline
Unemployment and Minorities

Further ways to refine your keyword search: Boolean operators

Many search facilities employ particular rules to help you to refine your search and to find the most relevant sources as efficiently as possible.

The most common rules for linking words are provided by **Boolean operators**. These are simple and straightforward to use and almost universal. But beware – frustratingly, some databases use their own operators and logic sequences and do use Boolean operators. Still, if you learn how to use any database then it is easier if you have understood Boolean operators and the logic which lies behind them.

Boolean operators are the words:

AND
OR
NOT
NEAR

These words are termed logical operators. Each denotes a particular type of logic which the search facility will use when you employ these terms within a search.

Using the AND operator

AND is used when you want to find material which *must* contain more than one word which you have specified.

So, as above, if you want to look at how levels of education affect use of technology, you would want to look at material which links the two. You could use the keywords and operator:

education AND technology

This would *only* find material which contained *both* terms, which is pretty much what you would want. If you did not use the AND operator, the search engine would look for all sources with the word education within them and all sources with the word technology in them. This would obviously result in many sources which are irrelevant to your particular concern.

You can add more terms. If you wanted, for example to look at how levels of education affected women's use of technology particularly, you could extend the number of keywords used and linked by the operator, for example:

education AND technology AND women

This would then only find material with all three words in it.

Using the OR operator

OR is used when you are using a number of RELATED terms; for example, levels of education can be measured by numbers of qualifications, so you might want to use this term in your search too. In which case you could use the keywords and operator:

education OR qualifications AND technology

This would find all the available material with both the words education and technology within it *and* all material with both the words qualifications and technology.

Using the NOT operator

NOT is used when you want to definitely exclude a term or concept. For example, you may be interested in how women use different sorts of technology but you are not interested in how or why they watch television, so you want to definitely exclude this form of technology from your search. You could therefore use the keywords and operator:

education AND technology AND women NOT television

This would then ensure that your search did not include any material which included the word television. Be careful when using the NOT operator. There might, for example, be some interesting material which specifically mentions that it is not looking at women's use of television – under this search, because the word television was excluded – this document would be rejected by the search tool.

Using the NEAR operator

NEAR is used when you want two or more keywords to appear close to each other in the text so that it is clear that the two concepts are indeed linked. So a piece which mentioned women and also mentioned technology, but did not link these two concepts particularly closely, would be more likely to be rejected by the search tool. So, for material which closely links two or more words, you could use the keywords and the operator NEAR, for example:

women NEAR technology

Determining the sequence of logic by using brackets

Sometimes Boolean logic can get quite complex because you can refine your search by combining a number of operators in the same search. Imagine, for example, that you are using a number of related words in your search. You could just employ all of these in some kind of list as below:

women OR females AND education NEAR technology NOT television OR TV

This is quite complicated and not very clear or logical. By using brackets, however, to 'group' concepts, you can determine exactly what you want the search tool to find. You could, for example, use brackets to 'group' (women OR females) and also to 'group' (television OR TV). Then your search is made more logical and would look like this:

(women OR females) AND education NEAR technology NOT (television OR TV)

The search tool will then immediately look for all materials with the word women and the word female when either is found in a website which closely links the concepts of both women and education with the concept of technology. Furthermore it will reject all material which refers to television or which refers to TV.

TOP TIP

When using Boolean operators make sure that you use CAPITAL LETTERS as we have done above. Not all search tools require this but some do, so it is good to get into the habit of capitalising these terms, just for when you will need to.

Refining your search using other search techniques

Using inverted commas

Many search tools will allow you to put words in **inverted commas** if you want it to look only for the **exact phrase** you have typed. The phrase 'digital divide' is one such phrase which should be put in inverted commas. Without these the search tool will look for all material with the word 'digital' and all material with the word 'divide' in it. But using 'digital divide' in inverted commas means that it will only search for pages that use that complete term, and use the words in that order.

You could also use inverted commas to find a complete phrase, for example:

'Life is beautiful' AND Trotsky

typed into Google immediately brought up exactly what we were looking for; Leon Trotsky's Testament written in 1940 in Mexico shortly before he died. He finishes this with the famous line 'Life is beautiful. Let the future generations cleanse it of all evil, oppression, and violence and enjoy it to the full.'

Alternative spellings/words

As long ago as 1887, Oscar Wilde, referring to similarities between Britain and North America, wrote: 'We have really everything in common with America nowadays except, of course, language'. In the intervening years that language gap has widened so when using search tools that purport to use the English language – be careful – it might use American English!

It is always a good idea to use **alternative spellings** of words where you know these exist – some words like *organization* and *organisation* have both spellings widely accepted, words like *colour* and *color* will be spelt differently by British and American writers and in each case both spellings should be used.

And remember that there are many **alternative words** which are different across the Atlantic – *cells* and *mobiles, bonnets* and *hoods, trunks* and *boots* – while well-used terms in their countries of origin, they mean very different things depending on whether you are using American or British English. Do you know all the alternative definitions these have in the American or British English?

Using a wildcard

Wildcards can be used to substitute for one or more letters in a keyword. This can be very useful – especially where spellings differ by one letter only.

Wildcards use the asterisk symbol * as a substitute for one or more letters – these asterisks can symbolise any letter or combination of letters depending on whether they are at the end or in the middle of a word. Take for example the word *organisation*. As we saw above, there are two accepted spellings which differ by the use of a z or an s – so why not use the wildcard and write:

*organi*ation*

This will now capture both spellings of the word as the asterisk in the middle of the word could be a substitute for any letter.

Wildcards can also be used to capture *different* words which again differ by only one letter. Imagine you are conducting your search on women's use of technology. You could use the wildcard in the following way:

wom*n

The search tool will now find all material with *women* and also with *woman* in the text.

If you place the wildcard at the end of a word, it can substitute for a combination of letters. For example you could use the search term:

sociolog*

This would then pick up on all the alternative endings for this word, such as *sociology* or *sociological*. So the wildcard can be very useful indeed.

Do not overuse wildcards – you are usually allowed a maximum of two per keyword and they cannot replace the first three letters, so

cat* is OK but *c*ts* is not

To use a wildcard too early in the word leaves too many possibilities, e.g. *c*ts* could mean *cats, cuts* or *cots.*

Using a dictionary or thesaurus

We have expressed the importance of owning a good dictionary at many points throughout this book. This could be a general dictionary or one which is specialist to your subject. When constructing searches and keyword diagrams and you are looking for RELATED WORDS and alternative spellings, dictionaries and thesauruses can prove invaluable.

Reading around the subject

There's really no substitute for reading around a subject before you begin to conduct a focused search in that subject area. How can you be expected to know the relevant words, sources of data and specialist information sources which you can use if you know very little about the subject in the first place?

Do some initial, general reading to start with, to get you thinking about the subject area and how it has been researched in the past, what theories are connected with it, who are the most relevant writers and theorists, and which organisations, websites, etc. are the best sources of data and information in that particular area of expertise.

78

Other types of searches

Searches do not always have to be conducted by keyword, you can also:

- Search by author – to find everything which a particular author has written.
- Search by institution – some databases allow you to search for material published by a particular institution.
- Search by title – if you know the title of the book or report which you are seeking, or if you are looking for all material in which particular key terms appear in the title.

Using bibliographies to find information sources

You can also use the bibliographies of books or articles to alert you to useful sources for your research. If you have found a particularly relevant piece of work then check the bibliography for other sources of information which you might want to read for yourself. This is why we construct bibliographies after all!

TOP TIP

Be systematic and focused in all your searches.

Ending your search

There is a lot of information available to the social scientist. You cannot read it all. Hopefully, by thinking about your question, focusing your search and using relevant keywords, you will find exactly what you are looking for as quickly and efficiently as possible. But remember, you cannot go on searching for ever. You should:

- Set a time limit for your search.
- Set a limit to the amount of data you want to collect.
- Set a limit to the amount of books which you want to consult.
- Make sure that the material you are using addresses the question.

When you have consulted a suitable number of sources THEN start to write. If you find you are having any problems completing your work because there are gaps in your knowledge, or you need more information, then you can go back and try to fill these in.

79

TOP TIP

Choosing your sources

It may seem obvious but make sure you have access to the right sources for the essay you have chosen. If you haven't – choose a different title. A *lecture* or a *textbook* chapter on the topic should alert you to what some of the key sources are.

Use *Internet sources* by all means but not at the expense of printed books and journals. Check Internet sources carefully.

In addition to locating sources on your specific area of interest, make sure you read some more *general works* relating to the topic so that you know where it fits into a wider framework.

After the first year *don't use general introductory textbooks* as key sources. They may have a chapter relating to the module you are studying which can be useful for preliminary reading but not for much else.

Use *primary sources*, including journal articles, as much as possible.

Chapter 10

Getting the most out of your library and the Internet

The library

Familiarising yourself with your local library

Libraries can be quite confusing places, so you need to get to know yours well. It is a good idea to browse around the different library floors which you will use and try to remember where the sections relevant to the social sciences are to be found, where the journals are kept and how the shelves are ordered so that you can make your way to the relevant section as easily as possible.

Libraries use different classification systems and you will need to find your way around these. One of the most often used is the Dewey Decimal System, which is explained below.

THE DEWEY DECIMAL SYSTEM

The Dewey Decimal System classifies human knowledge into 10 categories and each book is numbered according to the area of knowledge into which it has been classified. The main categories of interest to social scientists are as follows:

000   is the number given to works on computers, as well as works with a general theme such as encyclopaedias and reference books
100   refers to philosophy and psychology
200   refers to books on religion
300   refers to books classed as belonging to the social sciences
900   refers to geography and history

Of course not all books fit neatly into these categories – what about historical sociology or social geography? Categorising books is not an exact science.

Whichever category new books are classified into, they are then given class marks relevant to their broad area and these broad classes are subdivided into 10 further areas (or 100 sub-classes) and each of these is divided again into 10 (giving 1,000 sub-sub-classes). As you go further into the number, the classification becomes more specialised. For example:

300   refers to the Social Sciences
310   refers to statistics
314   refers to general statistics for Europe
314.1 refers to statistics for the UK

N.B. You will find a decimal point after each three digits, denoting that the classification number has moved into a further sub-category.

Also common is the Library of Congress System explained below.

THE LIBRARY OF CONGRESS SYSTEM

The Library of Congress Classification System separates all knowledge into 21 classes. Each class is then identified by a single letter of the alphabet. The main classes of interest to social scientists are as follows:

A GENERAL WORKS
B PHILOSOPHY. PSYCHOLOGY. RELIGION
C AUXILIARY SCIENCES OF HISTORY
D HISTORY (GENERAL) AND HISTORY OF EUROPE
E HISTORY: UNITED STATES
F HISTORY: AMERICA
G GEOGRAPHY. ANTHROPOLOGY. RECREATION
H SOCIAL SCIENCES
J POLITICAL SCIENCE
K LAW
L EDUCATION
Z BIBLIOGRAPHY. LIBRARY SCIENCE. INFORMATION RESOURCES
   (GENERAL)

Each of these broad classes is then broken down further by adding other letters. For example:

H	Social Sciences
HA	Statistics
HB–HC	Economics
HD–HG	Business
HM	Sociology
HQ	Family, Marriage, Sexual Life, Women, Feminism
HV	Social/Public Welfare, Alcoholism, Drug Abuse, Criminology
HX	Socialism, Communism, Anarchism

More specific topics are then identified by the addition of numbers. For example:

HM435–477	History of sociology. History of sociological theory
HM481–554	Theory. Method. Relations to other subjects
HM621–656	Culture
HV6001–7220.5	Criminology
HV7231–9960	Criminal justice administration

Searching for books

Books on specific topics are not always easy to find. Libraries have incomplete collections and there are often errors and omissions in their electronic catalogues, so it is worth being persistent and coming at the search from a number of angles.

Working with the library staff

Library staff are a source of support and help which the undergraduate does not often use. Libraries will have staff which specialise in your subject area.

They will be able to give you help and advice about looking for books, using electronic catalogues and the Internet. They will also know which databases and journals that the library subscribes to in your subject area. You should get to know who your subject librarian is and how to contact them.

For most undergraduate study

At undergraduate level you should not be directed to read any books which are not available in your university's library, so this should be your first point of call when searching for specific books which have been recommended to you. Library catalogues should allow searches by subject, by author, by title and also by keyword.

As electronic catalogues are not infallible, do not be put off if you do not find the book you are looking for straight away. Try focusing your search from the beginning to put in all the information which you have available, then widen your search if you are unable to find the book on the system. Be very careful when entering author names and initials. These will have to be spelt absolutely correctly for the majority of catalogues to locate them.

Library classification systems can use very wide categories to catalogue their books by subject matter, so subject searches are often the least rewarding.

TOP TIP

Most library catalogues do not require you to enter the whole of a book title when searching for books, a few keywords should be sufficient – and this can save you a lot of time and energy!

Conducting more advanced research

If you are carrying out your own research, perhaps for a dissertation, or for post-graduate work, you will often want to use books which your library will not carry. So how do you go about finding these?

- Use the bibliographies of books, articles and reports which you have already acquired. Which books do they cite?
- Use a citation index – citation indices record all those books and articles which have been cited by other scholars in their work.
- Search a bibliographic database which records all books in print at that time.
- Search the catalogues of libraries other than your own university facility, especially the British Library or the US Library of Congress. These hold a copy of most books printed in the UK and the US respectively.
- Do all of the above to conduct a really systematic search for books.

The website for this book has links to, and more information on, relevant citation indices and bibliographic databases as well as links to the British Library and US Library of Congress on the Internet.

Getting the book off the shelf

Once you have found some relevant books, you must then locate the actual book itself. This should be an easy enough exercise but it is not always. First you have to familiarise yourself with your local library and the classification system which it uses. Even when you find the place on the shelf where the book should be it is not always the case that you will find it. Books can be out, can disappear or be put back in the wrong place. If you cannot find a book which should be stocked by the library then report this as missing. The library staff will then search for the item for you.

If you cannot find the exact book you want, there may well be other relevant texts and you could look at the books nearby which will be classified similarly.

What if your library does not stock the book you want to read?

- You could try another library – check out whether you have visiting rights at nearby university libraries.
- Ask your own library to order the book for you on inter-library loan – but bear in mind you will most likely be charged for this.

TOP TIP

Start looking for books and planning your work well before the deadline for submission – the chances of finding the best books close to a deadline will be greatly diminished.

The Internet

Electronic searches

The advent of the Internet and the World Wide Web has dramatically changed the way we conduct searches. Prior to its adoption by most information providers as a tool for dissemination of their material, information largely came in 'hard copy', i.e. printed formats. Some information, such as copies of old newspapers and government documents, was made available on microfiche – large sheets of acetate on which papers and information were copied in microscopic print – special boxes with magnifying lenses had to be used to read these. It is only in the past decade that substantial amounts of information have been available in any kind of electronic format. In the vast majority of cases the researcher had to physically travel around the country, and sometimes the world, to search libraries and visit specialist archives for relevant statistical data and to get copies of the latest research. The widespread use of the Internet, however, has changed all that.

85

In the space of little more than a decade a whole range of information has become available through the Internet and the World Wide Web. Many library catalogues are now accessible as web-based documents, national and local government bodies have placed a great deal of data on the web and there are many documents, databases, video and audio-files which can all be accessed through computers. This has had an impact on research, not only making information much easier and faster to retrieve, but also by widening the scope of information which is readily available. A lot of information that was gathering dust in cellars has now been electronically 'captured' and placed on the web for all to access and use. This means that our research can be richer and more widely informed than ever before.

Look, for example, at the Moving Here website (http://www.movinghere. org.uk/) which was launched in the UK in 2003. This brings together National Archives of photographs, video and audio-clips, personal histories and official documents concerning migration to the UK over the past 200 years. The site also allows personal migration histories to be traced and for web-users to add their own migration stories to the site.

There are a number of ways to find information on the Internet:

1 If you have the exact address of the website, you can type this into whichever web browser that you are using. The exact address of the website is known as the URL which is short for Uniform Resource Locator. This will take you to straight to the site which you need. Take care to write URLs accurately; they are case-sensitive, so you cannot use capitals instead of lower-case and vice versa. They will often include colons and other symbols and these also have to be accurately entered. If you make any mistake you will not get through to the desired page.

2 If you do not have the exact address for the page which you want you can use the Search facility which is built into your web browser. When you log on to the Internet you will be taken to your home page. There will be a Search facility on this page – this is basically a box which has been left blank into which you will type your search terms. Your browser will then find a number of relevant sites for you.

3 If you want a more refined search you can use a 'search engine' to find sites for you. Search engines are databases which are specifically designed to find relevant Internet content. They are constantly updating themselves and look for the latest sites which they consider most fit your particular needs. They can link to literally millions of Internet websites, so you need to learn to use them to get the most focused search possible.

4 One way to ensure that your search is as focused as possible is to use a specialist web-based database. There are a number of these which cater for the needs of social scientists.

How to get the most out of your web browser

In recent years computer technology and the Internet have developed to such an extent that moving images and sound files have become a feature of many Internet sources. These can be very useful to the sociologist and you should consider using these as well as more text-based webpages. To play video and audio-files on your computer you will probably have to download some 'plug-ins'. These are pieces of computer software which 'plug' straight into your computer and allow you to play video and audio-files straight away. If you need these to play a file over the Internet you will be alerted to this and then, if you decide you want to use that particular plug-in, you just need to follow the instructions on the screen which will take you through the necessary process for downloading to suit your particular computer operating system. You will be able to download free versions of the software – but these may be old versions or might not give you access to all the software's facilities. They will be adequate though, although there will be an opportunity to purchase the most up-to-date version at some cost.

Whenever you 'visit' a webpage the links which you have visited will appear on your computer screen in a different colour. In a long and complicated search this can usefully alert you to the fact that you have already looked at a particular site and do not need to re-visit it.

You can save any type of file on to your computer as long as you have enough file-space. Place your mouse over any file, image or webpage and click using the right mouse button. This will give you a number of options, one of which is to save the file. You then just have to choose where you would like the file saved. See Chapter 11, Managing Information.

N.B. These files can be quite large, so do not download them if your computer does not have sufficient memory.

How to get the most out of your search engine

Search engines are a little more sophisticated than web browsers. They trawl around the web looking for pages and place these in on-line directories. You then use their own on-line forms to help you to find sources relevant to your interests. They are dedicated to finding specific types of content, so they are better at categorising and ordering information. This means that you are likely to find the most relevant sources higher up the results list. The better search engines will let you know how many 'hits', i.e. webpages, that it has found and some will give a 'relevance rating' after each link. Search engines will often allow quite sophisticated searches and will utilise Boolean operators so that you can refine your search. Try out a few search engines and decide which you find most useful. Whichever search engine you decide to use, make sure you are familiar with the operators which it recognises.

Search engines improve and change all the time, so we have not recommended any particular one. However, you will find an up-to-date list of quality search engines on the website associated with this book which you can try out at your leisure.

TOP TIP

You can change your homepage quite easily and some people choose to open their web browser directly into a search engine of their choice.

Use the Help function on your web browser to show you how to change your homepage.

Chapter 11

Managing information

If you carry out your research strategy successfully you will amass an awful lot of material. You should be as systematic in how you log and file this information as you have been at collecting it in the first place. You never know when you will again need the material you have collated and if you have dealt with it correctly you will be able to refer to it again at any time. Make the most of the information you collect – after all, you have expended a lot of thought and energy in getting your searches right in the first place.

We have all seen students with incredibly messy desks, with files all over the place and notes stuck into books. Strangely enough, this is not the best way to organise your material. The rest of this part looks at how you can manage large amounts of data and notes. By managing the information you collect in as tidy and efficient a manner as possible you will write better essays, as your notes, data, etc. will be better organised and so will your thoughts.

Trust us on this – we have many years of research experience behind us!

Logging searches and organising information

Some of the most frequently made mistakes by novice researchers are:

- making notes without properly recording the source of the material;
- taking quotes without properly recording the page/s from which the quote was lifted;
- not recording all the information which is needed to construct an accurate bibliography;
- forgetting what searches they have already made;
- conducting searches without recording when these were carried out;
- forgetting what databases/library catalogues, etc. have already been consulted;
- not recording how they found the material, e.g. the library classification number or the location of the website;

- only recording the homepage of the website and not the exact webpage used;
- forgetting which keywords they used to find information.

All these mistakes can waste the researcher a lot of time and involve them in:

- not knowing where material came from, so having to find it again, or worse still not being able to use the material at all if they cannot find it again;
- having to reread large chunks of books to find out where quotes were located in the text;
- having to relocate the original source to find out where, when and by whom it was published;
- running searches and then discovering that they have duplicated a search which they conducted some time ago, and worse still finding that this was a dead end then and still is;
- not knowing when a search was conducted, so not knowing when it should be updated to look for newly published material;
- having to search again from scratch for material they have already consulted but want to look at again;
- having to trawl through various links within websites to relocate the exact page which they found useful some time ago;
- re-using keywords which were no good in the first place!

But do not despair – all these frustrating *faux pas* can be avoided by following the advice which we set out below. First we stress the importance of *logging every search which you make*, systematically and with care. Even if the search was not fruitful – if you have it logged, you will avoid forgetting that it did not work and duplicating a piece of research which was a waste of time in the first place! On page 96 we look at how you should *take accurate notes* which include the page numbers of any ideas or quotes you take down and including full bibliographical references for every source you consult.

How to log your searches

Devise a form in which you can log all the searches that you make. This can be a paper form which you then physically file away, or this could be an electronic form which you keep on your computer. The beauty of using an electronic form is that you can copy and paste information which you find electronically directly into your form, and then from your form directly into your work. Copying and pasting, rather than copying by hand can save a lot of time *and* ensure that the information is accurately copied – transcribing long URLs onto paper forms can be especially time-consuming and likely to include mistakes.

The information which you will definitely need in your search log will be:

1 The purpose of the search.
2 The date which you conducted the search – remember two months down the line you might want to update it and if you know when you first carried out the search you can then limit your search from the last date you consulted that particular source to the present date.
3 Where you carried out the search – this may seem obvious but you can easily forget, for example, which library you used for a particular search.
4 In which database/catalogue, etc. you conducted the search – for example which journal or electronic source you used.
5 The date range which you used – a lot of databases allow you to restrict your search and only look for material published in certain years or months and you will need to keep a record of this.
6 Fields searched – did you for example conduct a keyword search or a search by author, institution or title?
7 Keywords used – including all operators.
8 The results of your search – the number of hits on a website, or books in the library which you found.
9 Which material you decided to use – including full bibliographical details.
10 Where you have filed the material itself or the notes you have made on the material.

In addition you might want to include a space for:

● Making your own notes about the search, on, for example, how successful the search was, or how you might refine it in the future.
● Listing the material you decided not to use.

Recording all this information at this stage might seem a bit arduous – but it will certainly save you much time and frustration in the end, so it is worth putting in the effort at this point to save you lots more effort at a later date.

A suggested format for your search log could be as shown in Figure 11.1.

Search log for:	
Date	
Location	
Source	
Date range	
Fields	
Search terms	
Results	
Used	
Locator	
Bibliographical details	
Filed in	
Notes	

Figure 11.1 *Search log*

A downloadable version of this form can be found on the Studying Society website. It is written in Word so can easily be edited to your liking.

An example of a completed search log is in Figure 11.2.

Search log for: Essay on the Digital Divide Oct 2004	
Date	12.09.04
Location	University of Liverpool Library
Source	Library catalogue – entire collection
Date range	N/A
Fields	Keywords
Search terms	Gender AND technology
Results	28 books
Used	Green and Adam (2001)
Locator	HQ1178.G79 – Sydney Jones Library
Bibliographical details	Green E. and Adam A. (eds) (2001) Virtual gender: technology, consumption and identity London: Routledge
Filed in	Notes in home computer files C://university/sociology/year3/Digital Divide/greenadam
Notes	Useful books were nos. 2, 5, 7, 13, 16, 18, 19, 21 Only one book (2) not on loan, all others ordered

Figure 11.2 *Completed search log*

A completed search log such as in Figure 11.2 will mean that you have all the information you need to hand, whenever you require it.

Chapter 12

Reading strategies

Now you have located your material and logged your searches you will have to read what you have found and take notes.

When devising a strategy for reading it is important to consider the purpose of your reading, and look at this for each specific piece which you have located. The purpose for your reading will, to a great extent, determine what sort of reading you will be engaged in. People read newspapers, for example, in a very different way from the way they read theoretical pieces or novels.

Newspapers can be skim read to glean bits of information which are important to the reader. The reader will often flick through the pages to find articles of interest, and it is certainly not unheard of for people to go straight to the back of a paper in order to read the sports pages first – and then to look at how the team they support is doing before reading any other material. It is not unusual for people to skip whole sections of newspapers if that part of the news is not interesting to them.

On the other hand, we do not read this way when we are reading theoretically informed and engaged academic work. It would be very unusual to read a complete newspaper from start to finish, giving each article and advertisement equal attention – after all, newspapers are written as 'bits' of information with headings, sub-headings and images to help you to decide which subject each piece is engaged with. The links are not made between one article and another. Academic debate and theoretical argument are quite the opposite.

Complicated theoretical arguments will often have to be followed from introduction to conclusion. Consider what a good piece of academic work will include.

When constructing an academic argument it is important to:

- Make your argument clear.
- Support your argument with evidence.
- Link different points.
- Construct a piece with an introduction, substantive section and a conclusion.

Within an academic piece of work:

- the introduction explains what the piece will address and how;
- the substantive section presents an argument or set of arguments with supporting evidence in the form of data and logical arguments;
- the conclusion interprets the material presented and explains its meaning.

So, if you are reading academic literature, it is much more likely that you will have to read the piece throughout in order to understand:

- what the author intends to do;
- the main points that the author makes;
- how each point links together;
- the meaning the author assigns to the material;
- the conclusions which are drawn from the material.

Textbooks, edited collections, encyclopaedias and readers are all differently structured. You will be able to dip in and out of these to find the particular parts you are interested in.

So the *type* of material which you are reading will determine how it is read. You should also consider, however, the *purpose* for which you are reading any piece.

There are a number of ways in which you can approach your reading:

- to get an overall impression of the subject;
- to find a specific piece of data;
- to understand key theoretical points.

Consider why you are reading a piece of work

Are you reading to get an overall impression of the subject?

If you are reading a piece in order to get a general impression of the subject area or to find some sort of background and general context in which to place your work, then you will need to:

- Decide what general area you are interested in.
- Look at chapter headings or in the index to help you get to the sections which you need.
- Skim read these sections to get the general gist of the subject area rather than look for detailed points.
- Only read the relevant sections.

You will probably not have to carry out a close reading in order to do this, even though the piece itself might be written as a closely considered argument.

Are you reading in order to find specific pieces of data?

If you are reading something to find specific bits of data or points of information you will probably be reading a report, rather than a closely argued, theoretical piece. In this case you will be able to:

- Use the table of contents or list of tables to go straight to the relevant sections.
- Look only at the relevant sections as your own work will be providing a context for the information and an understanding of the issues.

Are you reading in order to understand a theoretical argument?

If you are reading in order to better understand a theory or complex argument then you will need to carry out a close and thorough reading of the text. You will need to:

- Closely follow the order of the book in order to understand the author's logical reasoning.
- Read the introduction to see where the author is intending to take their argument.
- Read the conclusion in order to clarify the main points which the author is attempting to make.
- Take notes which help you to understand the author's main argument, and interpretation.
- Consider whether the argument in the piece is adequately supported by its logic or empirical data.

Taking notes

How you take notes is very much up to you and you will develop your own style; but there are a number of tips which you might want to take into consideration:

- Always **take full bibliographical references** for each piece you read – you will need these if you decide to use the material and it saves a lot of time if you do not have to go back to look for it.
- **Note how you can get hold of that particular piece again** in case you want to check something – so keep a note of the library classification

and the library from which it was borrowed, or make sure that you have the exact URL for a website, or note where the particular piece you have used has been filed.

- As you read through a piece, noting its main points, **keep a record of the page numbers** on which the point was made – this makes it easier for you to check again and it is a good idea to cite in your work the page numbers where key points are made. You would always have to do this for quotes, or for tables and diagrams, but you should also consider whether this would be appropriate when you refer to important points which the author makes.
- If you are reading a text closely then **read it more than once**. The first time should be to get the gist of the argument – where the author is going with the piece, and what perspective he or she is using. In subsequent readings you should note:
  - ❍ the author's key arguments;
  - ❍ how the author constructs their argument;
  - ❍ what questions the author asks;
  - ❍ how the author attempts to answer these questions;
  - ❍ what evidence the author uses to support their points;
  - ❍ how an argument is logically constructed.
- Do not take everything an author writes as necessarily valid and properly argued. Instead challenge and question the author's assumptions and arguments. Evaluate the material by considering its strengths and weaknesses. Note:
  - ❍ How well are different points made?
  - ❍ Are the arguments convincing?
  - ❍ How well does the evidence used support the points made?
  - ❍ Does the logical argument stand up to scrutiny?
  - ❍ Is there anything missing from the piece?
  - ❍ Could it be improved in any way?

You will now have cast a critical eye over each piece which you have read and you will be better able to see where each fits into your own work, and what contribution it can make to an understanding of the subject.

By not only reading the text but also analysing and evaluating its usefulness, you will ensure that you better understand everything that you have written.

Keeping records

Try to file all your information and notes as you take them – whether these are physical pieces of paper or computer-generated.

Files and Folders

Filing is a skill, and as with any skill must be practised regularly before you get it right. The key to good filing is to use plenty of folders and files which stack neatly into each other. Whether this is accomplished in actual space with physical folders, or virtually in computer files, this stacking system is generally the most efficient way of storing and retrieving files. Consider filing in the following way:

- open a folder for each major subject area
    - open a file within this folder for each module you take within that major subject area
        - open a file within this one for each piece of writing within that module, place within it material that is useful, for example on:
            - keyword searches
            - useful material
            - important data
            - lecture notes
            - one file for notes taken
            - another file for your own writing

Now you should be able to find any piece of information and writing whenever you need it.

Your file structure might look something like this:

- criminology
- gender and crime
    - assessment one
        - keyword searches
        - gender and crime documents
        - gender and crime lectures
        - gender and crime data
        - gender and crime notes
        - gender and crime writing

Other filing tips

- Always keep more than one record of your computer files. Computers are notoriously unreliable and are always crashing and losing work – to keep only one set is playing with fire. You should consider keeping a set of your computer files:
    - on your own PC's hard-drive;
    - on the hard drive space you are allocated at university;

○ on some kind of removable disk drive – like a flash drive or floppy which you can take around with you;

○ on your email system – email copies of your work to yourself, you can then retrieve them from your email inbox;

● Use the Favorites/Bookmarks function on your web browser so that you can link to all the useful webpages which you find. Use the filing system which your web browser gives you access to in order to store these links – by the end of an extended period of study you may have hundreds of websites which you use regularly or from time to time.

Chapter 13

Evaluating sources of information

OK! You have spent a lot of time tracking down information or knowledge, so now we must ask if it's any good. That word 'good', remember, requires us to specify some criteria before we can begin to tackle the question. So here are some criteria:

- relevance
- suitability
- trustworthiness

The first question you should ask of any piece of information or any source is:

- Is it relevant?

So, as we have already emphasised, the first step in any study or research is to work out what your goals are. Then you can decide if your source is relevant. If it isn't, don't waste time on it. Except . . .

Except that you may often come across something that might be relevant to a different question to the one you are pursuing at the moment. Don't waste time on it now, but you should make a note of it as it might save you some time in the future.

The next question should be:

- Is it suitable?

'Suitable' is another of those evaluative words that we have to be careful of. What we have in mind here is whether the source or the information is suitably detailed for your purposes. For instance, suppose you are writing an essay on something to do with the causes of criminal behaviour and you want to put in a paragraph on unemployment. Now you would probably find more than enough ideas for a few sentences in an introductory sociology textbook. But if you were writing a whole essay on unemployment then you would need some more detailed sources. But beware of being swamped by information that is too detailed or two advanced to be of much help to you.

The most important question to ask of any source though is:

- Can I trust it?

We will begin again with the example of choosing a university. What sources of information did you consult when trying to reach a decision? Teachers, parents, friends, newspaper league tables, university and departmental brochures, websites, open days? Did you give any thought to how trustworthy these different sources of information were?

By 'trustworthy', we don't mean to imply that any of your sources were dishonest: we are simply concerned with whether you can rely on the information that they gave you. Your Dad might have had a good time at the University of X 20 years ago, but is that information of any value to you now? Your friend, Sarah, has a big sister who raves about the Department of Geography at the University of Y, but is that any help when you want to study Criminology?

These questions raise issues of relevance again and also of currency – how up to date is the information? Does it apply to the situation you are facing now?

Were you impressed by the league tables you read in the national newspapers about the performance of different university departments? Did you really understand what all those different measures meant and did you think about whether they would actually affect your experience as a student?

Scepticism

What you should do is adopt a *sceptical* approach to the various sources of information to which you are exposed. Dictionaries out again! Scepticism = 'inclination to question the truth or soundness of accepted ideas, facts, etc.; critical; incredulous' (OED).

A story is told of Pyrrho, the founder of Pyrrhonism (which was the old name for scepticism). He maintained that we never know enough to be sure that one course of action is wiser than another. In his youth, when he was taking his constitutional one afternoon, he saw his teacher in philosophy (from whom he had imbibed his principles) with his head stuck in a ditch, unable to get out. After contemplating him for some time, he walked on, maintaining that there was no sufficient ground for thinking he would do any good by pulling the man out. Others, less sceptical, effected a rescue, and blamed Pyrrho for his heartlessness. But his teacher, true to his principles, praised him for his consistency.

(Russell, 1928: 11–12)

Now, like Russell, we would not advocate such an extreme position as that of Pyrrho but we would recommend that you approach all sources of information with the attitude that, whilst you are open to persuasion, you are not going to be easily convinced. In other words always ask why you should believe what you are reading or hearing or seeing – what is the evidence, what is the logic? (We suggest that you don't take this approach in your private life – you will be a pain to be around if you are constantly challenging everything anyone says to you.) Nevertheless,

> 'as long as men are not trained to withhold judgement in the absence of evidence, they will be led astray by cocksure prophets, and it is likely that their leaders will be either ignorant fanatics or dishonest charlatans'.
>
> (Russell, 1950: 42)

Russell recommends (and we would too) a position between the extremes of scepticism and dogmatism in which we need evidence before we can say that we know something but that even when we have evidence we recognise that there is an uncertainty about our knowledge. What we think we know may turn out not to be true, or not to be forever true or not to be true under all conditions. As Russell says, 'instead of saying "I know this", we ought to say 'I more or less know something more or less like this' (ibid.: 43).

Critically evaluating an author's work

There will be times when you need to look at an author's work very closely in order to evaluate its contribution to a subject under study. This will involve a very close reading of the text but will also involve you in questioning that author's assumptions and the logic of their argument. It is a good idea to skim read the work initially and then to go back to it and raise important questions about the author, their interest in the subject, and the work itself.

Ask the following questions of each author which you read:

1 Who is the author and what are their qualifications for writing about this topic?
   ● Where are they located?
     Authors will generally write from a perspective which is familiar to them, so it makes a difference which part of the world they are from. Are they writing from an African perspective, from North or South America? Are they European or Chinese? This may make a difference – they may be writing using the insights which their particular culture or national background gives them. This might be important to your work and you need to assess this. At the very least if someone is writing from a

EVALUATING SOURCES OF INFORMATION

particularly Western perspective you must be aware that this is the case and not generalise their work to other, non-Western, cultures.

- What is the affiliation of the author?

  Consider whether the author is attached to a university, a government organisation, a policy think-tank or even a magazine or newspaper?

  A person's affiliation may well affect what they write. Generally an academic attached to a university should have complete freedom of expression and be able to write exactly what they want, but those who are employed by other institutions may have to toe an institutional line. Certainly members of policy think-tanks will have a particular take on the world and this will be reflected in the organisation which they have chosen to write for. Certain organisations employ a particular reading of world issues. It is well known, for example, that the Institute for Economic Affairs in Britain is linked to neo-liberal and conservative ways of thinking, whereas the organisation SHELTER which is concerned with housing rights, has a more liberal outlook.

  Check out the affiliation and interests of different organisations by consulting their websites.

- What theoretical perspective do they use?

  Authors do not always make their theoretical perspective clearly known in everything that they write. If an author is less well known you may have to uncover their particular perspective by a close reading of the text. Look for key terms they use which would help to reveal their particular standpoint. Look also for what the author takes for granted and does not question or explain – this can often reveal their particular standpoint.

  If an author is well known in their subject area it will be much easier to uncover the perspective from which they are working. You can do this by looking at how other people explain their work, with which people they co-write or by looking at what they have written in the past and how their work has developed.

- When was the work written?

  It is important to look at the date when the work was first published. Published work sometimes gets dated very quickly as new work comes out which responds to and builds upon previous material. On the other hand, recently published material is not necessarily better than older material, but research carried out in, say, 1973 needs to be set in context.

2 What are the main assumptions which the author is making?

Don't take an author's arguments for granted. Try to develop a critical stance towards their work. Question their assumptions, interrogate their argument and assess the relevance of the evidence they present to back up their assertions. In order to do this you should note:

- the main points which the author is making;
- how these are supported;
- if the author is making a logical argument – does it hold up to scrutiny;
- whether the author presents relevant empirical material;
- whether the evidence presented supports the points made;
- if the author is expressing facts or opinion;
- if the author cites other scholarly works in the text.

Look at the following example to see how asking these sorts of questions can reveal something about an author's perspective:

3 What is the author's main purpose?

4 Who is or was the intended audience of the source?

Example:
A CRITICAL READING OF CHARLES MURRAY'S *THE EMERGING BRITISH UNDERCLASS* (1990)

Main point
- A potentially violent and problematic underclass is present, and growing, in the UK.

The argument
- Among other points, Murray argues that increased rates of illegitimacy signal an increase in an underclass in Britain.

What evidence does the author present?
- In 1960, 5% of all births in Britain were to unmarried women; this rose to 28% by 1990.

Does the evidence support the argument?
- No, there are various ways of interpreting the data. Not all unmarried mothers could be said to belong to an underclass: they may be unmarried but cohabiting, may have professional jobs or be relatively wealthy.

Is the author expressing facts or opinion?
- The writing is very opinionated in parts. Some empirical material is presented but there are also many un-evidenced assertions and his interpretation of the data presented is open to challenge.

Does the author cite other scholarly works in the text?
- There is no Bibliography.

What perspective is Murray coming from?

■ The book is written from a particularly conservative, neo-liberal standpoint for a popular audience, rather than an academic audience.

Clues

■ The book's publisher is the Institute for Economic Affairs – a right-wing think-tank.

■ His book was sponsored by *The Sunday Times*. In 1990 the editor expressed support for the British Conservative Party.

■ The book was serialised in *The Sunday Times*.

■ The writing uses a dramatic tone rather than considered academic objectivity. He writes: 'I arrived in Britain earlier this year, a visitor from a plague area come to see whether the disease is spreading' Murray (1990: 3).

The answers to these questions would lead us to question Murray's work and the validity and objectivity of his arguments.

A note on Internet sources

Everything we have said about evaluating information should also be applied to sources of information which you find on the web. In fact you should take extra care with web-based sources. Remember that anyone can publish on the Internet and that it hasn't necessarily been checked by anyone.

Remember too that anyone can be who they like on the Internet and that people can (and do) lie. Did you know, for example, that www.whitehouse.org is very definitely NOT the official site of the US government. Check it out and see – it LOOKS very professional and authoritative – but it is in fact a spoof website. Now try to find the OFFICIAL website for the US government. How do you know that this is the real one?

So with Internet sources you have to be particularly vigilant. The first thing to ask is this:

● Is the material available elsewhere in a printed version?

As we pointed out in an earlier section, some of the material available on the Internet is simply printed material available in a different, and often more convenient, format. On-line versions of respectable journals and government reports can simply be treated in the same way as their paper counterparts. But remember that all is not always what it appears to be on the Internet and something that looks like a respectable journal could be a propaganda organ for some dubious organisation. However, if you access the journal via your university's library website you should be able to rely on its authenticity.

We pointed out in the section on Internet sources that there are academic portals and guides to quality web-based sources. Sites found via these routes should also be reliable and it is best to treat anything else with extreme caution. If in doubt – consult your tutor.

There are certain checks which you can carry out to verify any Internet sources:

- Try to find out something about the person who wrote the webpage – what is their background, are they a well-known writer, what is their institutional affiliation, do they belong to a respectable organisation?
- Who is hosting the website? There will be clues to this in the URL. Any UK-based sites will have the suffix gov.uk if they are government hosted and ac.uk if they are held on a university server. If they are hosted by more generally used servers such as yahoo or hotmail they are more likely to be personal accounts and you should really subject them to scrutiny.
- Where do the links on the page lead? If the page is linked to more reputable sites then this is a good indication that the author of the site is linked to these organisations in other ways too.

Final thoughts

Triangulation is a term that is used in research methodology and, put simply, refers to the idea of looking at the same thing in different ways; so it might involve using a number of different sources or a number of different methods. The idea is that we get a better picture of something if we look at it from a number of different angles. All sources of information have their advantages and their disadvantages. So we recommend that you bear in mind the basic idea of triangulation and look at as many different sources as possible.

Adopt a sceptical approach to your sources, be critical; just because something is published in a book, newspaper or website doesn't mean it is reliable or unproblematic. On the whole, information provided by 'experts' is likely to be more valid than that provided by those without any expertise in the particular area. But the 'experts' may not agree, so you cannot avoid making your own assessment of a particular topic and, as Russell remarked, 'even when the experts all agree, they may well be mistaken' (1928: 12).

Part IV

Researching society

INTRODUCTION

In this book we are mainly concerned with locating knowledge or information that is already available in some form. At an undergraduate level you will not usually be expected to carry out original research although you might be asked to carry out a small project in order to learn how to conduct research. As well as providing a grounding for any future research that you might carry out, it is important for you to know something about research methods in order that you can make an informed evaluation of the methods used in the studies that you read.

Quantity and quality

A common distinction made when discussing research methods in the social sciences is between quantitative and qualitative methods. Basically the distinction is a simple one: quantitative methods produce data that can be expressed in a numerical form, whereas qualitative methods produce data that can only be expressed in a non-numerical way. Whilst these methods have their roots in different philosophical positions and you will find some people who will argue for the superiority of one over the other, we would urge you to think in terms of the advantages and disadvantages of each.

To begin with both approaches have a number of features in common: they both aim to explain or understand some aspect of social life and they try to do this by the systematic collection and analysis of empirical material.

Chapter 14

Quantitative research

Quantitative methods are typically associated with an approach known as *positivism*. Different authors define positivism slightly differently, but for us it refers to an approach to studying society which tries to emulate the methods of the natural sciences. Amongst other things, this entails the assumptions that:

- there exists a 'real' world which is independent of our understanding of it;
- we can discover that reality by means of empirical research;
- research can be conducted in an objective fashion free from the intrusion of the scientist's own values and emotions.

As a consequence of these assumptions positivism is only concerned with those things that can be verified by checking them against 'reality'. And to achieve objectivity this usually involves attempts to *measure* aspects of human behaviour and social life. This in turn usually involves privileging the collection of 'hard' data – that to which a numerical value can be assigned. A person's age, whether or not they have a job, whether they agree or disagree with a particular statement, is straightforward and factual – there is no room for disagreement (assuming the person is telling the truth!).

Another assumption that many writers associate with positivist approaches is that human behaviour and many aspects of human society can be seen as *determined*, that is as a product of some preceding cause. So a main preoccupation of positivist approaches is in attempting to discover *causal relationships* between *variables*.

A variable is simply an attribute of something or someone which can vary: a person's gender – whether they are a man or a woman – is a variable for example; so too is their age or whether they are married or not. At a societal level, the number of crimes reported to the police or the number of people registered as unemployed are also variables.

Having a measure of a single variable can be interesting and useful. We might know for example that the number of crimes reported to the police in England and Wales in the year 2003–2004 was 5.9 million. However, that information becomes much more useful if we can link it to another variable. For example, if we bring in the variable of time we can look at how last year's figures compare with those in previous years. Another variable we could bring in would be the country to which the figures refer. So, for example, we could compare the number of crimes reported in different countries in Europe.

Validity

So we can compare the 5.9 million crimes reported in 2003–2004 with the number reported in previous years and we can tell if crime is increasing or decreasing. Can we? No we cannot – remember that the 5.9 million refers to *crimes reported to the police* and not to *crimes committed*. What if in some years people *report* a greater percentage of crimes committed against them than in other years? This could easily happen – there might be a level of moral panic or fear raised around crime which motivates more people to report crimes to the police. This raises an issue which is a general problem in research – the problem of *validity*.

The issue of validity is concerned with whether or not a method of research or a particular measure is actually revealing what it appears to be doing. To grasp the idea think about a measuring device such as an electricity meter or a car's speedometer. The question of the validity or otherwise of these devices is concerned with whether or not they measure the amount of electricity consumed or the speed at which the car is travelling. When it comes to human behaviour, however, the issue of validity becomes much more complicated.

A classic issue concerns the attempts by psychologists to measure intelligence. To begin with there have been major debates over what the concept of intelligence actually refers to. Nevertheless, psychologists have devised various tests designed to measure intelligence levels which have been deployed in real situations to make decisions about people's lives. We might point out first of all that the idea that intelligence is a variable that can be quantified is a typically positivist one. But for our purposes here the interesting issues around the question of validity have arisen when intelligence tests have apparently shown that some groups of people are more intelligent than others. Questions have been raised about the objectivity of these tests and whether what they measure is not actually some neutral thing called intelligence but rather some abilities which are most likely to be possessed by white, educated men.

Reliability

Another major issue of particular concern to quantitative researchers is *reliability*. This refers to the consistency or stability of a particular interview schedule, questionnaire or other method of research. There are a number of different aspects to this, but if a questionnaire or other measure is reliable, then we expect it to give consistent results over time. If you have a set of bathroom scales that tell you that you weigh 10 stone one day but 9 stone the next you might be pleased but you would suspect that the scales were not very reliable, especially if the next day they suggested that your weight had gone up to 11 stone. On the other hand, if your scales consistently gave your weight, *and that of any one else who used them*, as 10 stone, then you couldn't fault them for reliability but you would be well advised to question their validity as a device for measuring weight!

In the study of society we need to ensure that our ways of measuring people's motivations and actions are equally reliable. What if a question was so badly constructed that its meaning was obscure – it could be interpreted differently by different people, or by the same person some weeks down the line. This would be an unreliable measure. Think about the collection of recorded crime statistics again. We would have to make sure that all people recording crime statistics were using the same definitions of the crimes they were recording – this is not as simple as it might seem. Do you know the difference between robbery and theft from the person?

Relationships between variables

Let us move on to a different issue. Assuming we have a valid measure of crime in a society, another variable that we could link it to is the level of unemployment. It would be reasonable to ask if there is a relationship (and again we are not talking romance here!) between the level of crime and the level of unemployment in a society. It is perhaps not unreasonable to expect that a society with a high level of unemployment will also have a high level of crime.

EXERCISE 14.1

Take a few minutes rest from reading at this point and write down a list of reasons why you might assume that a society with a high rate of unemployment would also have a high rate of crime. Or if you think that it is more reasonable to assume that a high level of unemployment would be found with a low level of crime write down your reasons for assuming that too.

Now you are very close to setting up what quantitative researchers call a *hypothesis*. A hypothesis is simply a proposition that can be tested by a piece of research; in this case the hypothesis is about what we expect to find when we look at the relationship between crime and unemployment rates. In the following example we have suggested that commonsense might provide us with a hypothesis; but why should we look at crime and unemployment in the first place?

Well, there might be a role for theory here and sometimes quantitative researchers may be concerned with testing a theory by *deducing* some propositions from it and checking them against the empirical data. You will find more on this in the next section. One famous theory in the criminological literature is that formulated by the American sociologist Robert Merton back in 1938 and building on Durkheim's concept of *anomie*. You can read about Merton's ideas in any textbook on criminological theory, but the main point for our purposes here is that he suggested that if people did not have access to legitimate means of achieving success in society (jobs, careers, businesses) then they could turn to illegitimate means such as crime.

So one way to *begin* to test Merton's idea would be to see if a society with a high level of unemployment (lack of access to legitimate means) also has a high level of crime (illegitimate means). Suppose we did find that to be the case? Has Merton's theory been proven to be correct? Well, no, because all we have established is that there is a relationship between crime and unemployment rates. It could be that having no work means that you have to turn to burglary to get what you want but it could equally be that if you are convicted of an offence you lose your job. In other words we haven't proven that the relationship between our two variables is a *causal* one or, if it is, which one is caused by the other – or in technical language, which is the independent variable (the one which is the cause) and which is the dependent variable (the effect).

Another Example:

Suppose a study shows that:

- Of 100 people attending a place of worship on a regular basis 20 were divorced.
- Of 100 people not attending a place of worship regularly 80 were divorced.

How would you represent the relationship between religion and divorce?

- Religious attendance causes reduced divorce – No
- Religious attendance leads to reduced divorce – No
- Religious attendance influences reduced divorce – No
- Religious attendance is associated with reduced divorce – Yes

What methods can we use to collect quantitative data?

Quantitative researchers don't only conduct research using official statistics; they sometimes have to gather the data themselves to begin with. Quantitative research typically uses questionnaires or interviews in which the questions are in a fixed format with a series of predetermined answers which the interviewer or the respondent can choose by, for example, ticking a box. The answers of all the respondents are then entered into a computer for statistical analysis. In Part V, we discuss the ways in which numerical data can be presented, including the use of tables, charts and graphs.

A good example of a large-scale survey is the National Survey of Sexual Attitudes and Lifestyles which was first carried out in Britain in 1990–1991 (Wellings *et al.*, 1994). A second survey was carried out in 1999–2001. The aim of these surveys was to gather information about people's sexual behaviour, their number of sexual partners, their use of contraceptive methods and so on. Such information is important in planning sexual health initiatives. The ideal would be to ask everyone in the country about their sexual behaviour. Obviously that would be very expensive and, if we did it for every topic we needed information about, impracticable as well. In place of the ideal, researchers study a *sample*. In the second National Survey of Sexual Attitudes and Lifestyles, a *sample* of just over 11,000 people was interviewed. That is still a lot of people but obviously much less than the adult population of the UK.

So interviewing a sample clearly saves money; but are the results any use? Can what we learn about the sexual behaviour of these 11,000 people tell us anything about the sexual behaviour of the rest of the population? What if the sexual habits of these people are completely different from those of the rest of us? Well, fortunately by using sophisticated sampling and statistical techniques (which we won't go into here) it is possible to draw a *random* sample of people that is *representative* of the whole *population* and the results of the research can then be used to give a fairly accurate estimate of what we would find out if we were able to interview everyone. When we use the term *population* here we are referring to everyone in a particular category – it might be all adults in the UK as in the example here but in another study it could be all higher education students, all infant school teachers, all bus drivers, all people earning £20,000–£29,000 or whatever category we were interested in.

A study that surveys the whole population is called a census. Because of the cost and the availability of accurate sampling procedures, censuses are rare and usually refer to studies of national populations carried out by governments (see Box overleaf).

113

THE UK NATIONAL CENSUS

Every 10 years since 1801 there has been a census in the UK. The last one took place in 2001 and cost around £255 million. The census includes every household and each person living there. Information is gathered about such things as the nature of the accommodation, the relationships of the people in the household, their age, gender, ethnic group, occupation, educational qualifications and so on.

The information is needed so that national and local government departments concerned with such things as transport, health, housing, education and so on can plan ahead.

You can find out more about the census at: http://www.statistics.gov.uk/census2001/default.asp

More issues with official statistics

Another example of a large survey is the British Crime Survey. But before we look at what that is we need to look at why it is necessary in the first place. At first glance it seems reasonable to ask how much crime there is in a particular society at a particular time; in practice it is not so easy as that. Rival politicians are always keen to claim that there is less crime when they are in government but criminologists know that it is not that simple.

Is the number of crimes recorded by the police a valid indicator of the number of crimes committed? The honest answer (not the one given by politicians) has to be 'we don't know but we have good reasons for believing not'. What are those good reasons? Well, to begin with, if someone is discovered to have committed a crime there is a possibility that they will be punished, so we can assume, not unreasonably, that those who have committed crimes will not list them on their curriculum vitae!

So we will have to depend on other people to tell us if a crime has been committed or not. Some crimes may be witnessed or will have a victim but in either case the occurrence of the crime may not be reported to the authorities. Again it is reasonable to assume that in at least some cases witnesses or victims, for example in cases of domestic violence, may be too frightened to report what has happened. In some cases, such as complex financial frauds, the victims – those who have been defrauded of their money may not even be aware of that fact. Some crimes, such as the possession of illegal drugs, do not have victims in the conventional sense and their discovery depends on the actions of law enforcement officers. In crimes such as burglary or car theft victims will presumably want, if they can, to claim on their insurance policy, if they have one. To do that they need first to have reported the crime to the police, so it would be reasonable to assume that reporting rates for such crimes are high. As the different examples we have given suggest, the answer to the question 'how valid is the level of crime recorded by the police as a measure of crime itself' will vary depending on the type of crime we are concerned about. The extent of murder, for example, will be more accurately known than the extent of criminal damage, as people are more likely to report murder to the authorities.

Furthermore, if a crime is reported it may not necessarily be recorded. A famous study of crime rates in neighbouring English counties a few years ago found that the differences in the recorded crime rate could largely be accounted for by differences in police recording practices rather than differences in criminal behaviour.

> 'Police forces across the country have been taking part in a huge hoax in which they have pretended to detect tens of thousands of crimes and have wiped from the records a mass of other petty crimes, a *Guardian* investigation has revealed. . . . Senior officers, most of whom claim to be unaware of the malpractice within their forces, have benefited from crime figures which credit them with a bogus success. Home Secretaries have repeatedly claimed false glory.'
>
> (*Revealed: how police fiddle crime figures*, Nick Davies,
> Thursday 18 March, 1999: *The Guardian*)

And if we add to this the possibility that the reporting behaviour of witnesses and victims and the activities of the police are likely to vary over time, then the issue becomes even more complicated.

Whilst social scientists have probably always been aware of some of the limitations of such statistics, it was in the 1960s that their use came under heavy scrutiny. It was pointed out that crime statistics were not a simple representation of 'reality' but were in fact (in a much over-used phrase) 'socially constructed' – that is they were the end result of many decisions made by such people as victims, witnesses, police personnel, jurors and magistrates. In other words crime statistics are a picture of our reactions to crime rather than an accurate representation of the number of crimes which take place.

A recent study has pointed out that 'Sexual violence, and rape in particular, is considered the most under-reported crime' and it continues:

A wide range of reasons for not reporting have been documented, the major ones being:

- not naming the event as rape (and/or 'a crime') oneself;
- not thinking the police/others will define the event as rape;
- fear of disbelief;
- fear of blame/judgement;
- distrust of the police/courts/legal process;
- fear of family and friends knowing/public disclosure;
- fear of further attack/intimidation;
- divided loyalty in cases involving current/ex-intimates; and
- language/communication issues for women with disabilities and/or whose first language is not that of the country where they were assaulted.

(Kelly *et al.*, 2005: 31–32)

Considerations of this sort have led criminologists to attempt to devise more accurate measures of crime. One has been the victim survey. First used in the 1960s, victim surveys such as the British Crime Survey have been used more regularly since the early 1980s alongside the traditional crime statistics. Originally taking place every two years, the British Crime Survey is now conducted annually and involves asking a random sample of people (currently around 40,000) about their experiences of victimisation over the previous 12 months. The aim is to arrive at a more valid measure of crime which has not been affected by reporting or recording decisions. The survey is a valuable source of information alongside the recorded statistics but does not replace them. A comparison of the coverage of the BCS and police recorded crime is given in Table 14.1.

In summary there are many advantages to using quantitative research methods:

- You can collect data from a large number of people.
- The answers can be processed using computers and standard statistical procedures.
- The results can be generalised to a population.

Table 14.1 *Comparison of the British Crime Survey and Police Recorded Crime*

The British Crime Survey	*Police Recorded Crime*
■ Starting in 1982, it measures both reported and unreported crime. As such it provides a measure of trends in crime not affected by changes in reporting, or changes in police recording rules or practices.	■ Collected since 1857. Provides a measure of offences which are both reported to and recorded by the police. As such they are influenced by changes in reporting behaviour and recording rules and practices.
■ Measures crime every two years.	■ The police provide monthly crime returns, and figures are published every six months.
■ Includes some offences the police are not required to notify to the Home Office.	■ Only includes 'notifiable' offences which the police are required to notify to the Home Office for statistical purposes.
■ The measure is based on estimates from a sample of the population. The estimates are therefore subject to sampling error and other methodological limitations.	■ Provides an indicator of the workload of the police.
■ Does not measure crime at the small area level well.	■ Provides data at the level of 43 police force areas.
■ Does not include crimes against: – those under 16 – commercial and public sector establishments – those in institutions.	■ Includes crimes against: – those under 16 – commercial and public sector establishments – those living in institutions.
■ Does not provide a measure of: – victimless crimes (e.g. drug, alcohol misuse) – crimes where a victim is no longer available for interview – fraud.	■ Measures: – victimless crimes – murder and manslaughter – fraud.
■ Collects information on what happens (e.g. when crimes occur, and its effects in terms of injury and property loss).	■ Collects information about the number of arrests, who is arrested, the number of crimes detected, and by what method.
■ Provides information about how the risks of crime vary for different groups.	■ Does not show which groups of the population are most at risk of victimisation.

From Mirrlees-Black *et al.* (1998)

Chapter 15

Qualitative research

There is a lot going on in our lives which cannot be expressed by a number. Even the longest of questionnaires can only tap into a small part of people's experiences. Do you remember the distinction that Wright Mills made between personal troubles and public issues? Statistics on a public issue such as crime, unemployment or divorce are certainly useful but they do not give us much of an insight into the ways in which these issues are experienced as personal troubles. Look at the following box.

EXTRACTS FROM *THE ROAD TO WIGAN PIER*, BY GEORGE ORWELL

The life of a single unemployed man is dreadful. He lives sometimes in a common lodging-house, more often in a 'furnished' room for which he usually pays six shillings a week, funding himself as best he can on the other nine (say six shillings a week for food and three for clothes, tobacco, and amusements). Of course he cannot feed or look after himself properly, and a man who pays six shillings a week for his room is not encouraged to be indoors more than is necessary. So he spends his days loafing in the public library or any other place where he can keep warm. That – keeping warm – is almost the sole preoccupation of a single unemployed man in winter. In Wigan a favourite refuge was the pictures, which are fantastically cheap there. You can always get a seat for fourpence, and at the matinee at some houses you can even get a seat for twopence. Even people on the verge of starvation will readily pay twopence to get out of the ghastly cold of a winter afternoon.

(Orwell, 1962: 71–72)

> We walked up to the top of the slag-heap. The men were shovelling the dirt out of the trucks, while down below their wives and children were kneeling, swiftly scrabbling with their hands in the damp dirt and picking out lumps of coal the size of an egg or smaller. You would see a woman pounce on a tiny fragment of stuff, wipe it on her apron, scrutinize it to make sure it was coal, and pop it jealously into her sack.
>
> (Orwell, 1962: 91)

> That scene stays in my mind as one of my pictures of Lancashire: the dumpy, shawled women, with their sacking aprons and their heavy black clogs, kneeling in the cindery mud and the bitter wind, searching eagerly for tiny chips of coal. They are glad enough to do it. In winter they are desperate for fuel; it is more important almost than food.
>
> (Orwell, 1962: 93)

Orwell was not of course a trained sociological researcher but in *The Road to Wigan Pier*, he gives an account of working-class life in England at a time of high unemployment in the 1930s which is based on methods used in qualitative research. He probably, in fact, did not think he was using a particular method of research and he certainly didn't do it systematically. But in order to understand 'working-class life', Orwell did what a qualitative researcher would do: he went off and talked informally to people, he observed them and to a certain extent shared their lives.

In quantitative research the fact that we share with the people we study the characteristic of being human is a problem, something that might get in the way of studying our subjects objectively. In qualitative research that shared humanity is treated as an asset. It means that we can develop an *understanding* of our subject matter that is not possible in the natural sciences. Max Weber, another of the 'founding fathers of sociology', pointed out that this depth of understanding carries a price in the loss of precision that it entails.

Qualitative research is rooted in a tradition that contrasts with that of positivism. Again this has been characterised in slightly different ways and has been given different names by different writers. Here we will use the term *interpretivism*. Interpretivism emphasises the differences between the subject matter of the social and the natural sciences.

As in Orwell's account, interpretivism stresses the need for rich description, to understand the particular social phenomenon concerned, a type of understanding that cannot be reduced to numbers. Only by getting close to people's lives and their social settings can we come to understand the meaning of those

119

lives. So measurement is of little interest to the qualitative researcher, although you will find that numbers are not entirely missing from their work. Nor is the qualitative researcher interested in variables and the relationships between them.

Qualitative researchers are certainly interested in change and in concepts relating to issues of time. However, commonly human action is not seen as determined by causal factors, as it is in the positivist approach, and instead the emphasis is on human agency and free will.

The issue of reliability is not of great concern in qualitative research. Indeed because each researcher is unique, as is each person, and social situation studied, no two pieces of research can ever be the same. The issue of validity in some form is usually a consideration, however, since the qualitative researcher will claim that there is some correspondence between their account and the social world they have studied. Some writers claim that a long-term qualitative research project will produce a more valid picture of a piece of social life than can be produced by a method such as a social survey, although demonstrating that validity may be more difficult.

EXERCISE 15.1

Consider the following:
How can you judge the validity of George Orwell's accounts of Lancashire life which are reproduced above?

Two final general points about qualitative approaches. The idea of doing value-free objective research is usually seen as an impossibility for the qualitative researcher: as a human being the researcher cannot deny his or her values and emotions. So in qualitative research great emphasis is placed on being reflexive, that is on trying to be aware of our assumptions and prejudices and taking account of the ways in which they might influence our research.

Qualitative researchers are usually less concerned with the issue of whether the groups or the people studied are representative of a broader population. In many areas it is impossible to achieve representative samples anyway – if you are studying delinquent gangs there is no way to draw up a random sample. We simply do not know enough about the extent and typology of juvenile gangs to make a representative sample possible. Nor can we know exactly who is a gang member and who is not – many gang members will not reveal this status to the researcher.

120

What methods can we use to collect qualitative data?

At the other extreme to the large social survey or census is the *life-history study*. As this term suggests, a life-history study is a focus on the experiences of one person. As Plummer notes:

> Usually, this is gathered over a longish period of time with gentle guidance from the researcher, the subject either writing down episodes of life or tape-recording them. At its richest, it will be backed up with keeping diaries, intensive observation of the subject's life, interviews with friends, the perusals of letters and photographs.
>
> (2001: 20)

In one example, Bogdan (1974) recorded approximately a hundred hours of interviews over a period of three months with the transsexual who he calls 'Jane Fry'. This resulted in about 750 pages of material when the tapes were transcribed (typed up into a computer document and printed off). This is a lot of material but it is still incomplete. Condensing the years of a person's life into a usable form will always involve some selection.

Other projects using qualitative research methods will involve detailed *interviews* with a small number of people. In contrast to quantitative interviews or questionnaires, such interviews will typically not employ fixed questions with predetermined answers. Instead the interviewer will begin with a list of topics that they wish to explore with the respondent, but they will also be alert to any other topics that the respondent might raise. The interviewer is free to pursue any line of questioning that the respondent is willing and able to allow. Usually these interviews will be tape recorded and then transcribed.

Another method that qualitative researchers may employ is *observation*. This means, of course, watching what people do. Actually, watching people can be very limited in what it can tell you. Suppose you see someone writing on a piece of paper in the library. Now they might well be writing an essay or taking notes for one; but equally they could be writing a letter, or compiling a shopping list. And if they are writing an essay, are they enjoying it, is it interesting, or are they just dashing off something at the last minute that they hope will be adequate? So most researchers in the social sciences use a form of participant observation.

This involves the researcher spending a long period of time in the social setting, or with the group that is being studied, observing what is going on, talking to the people involved and gathering any other data that might be helpful, such as documents relating to the group or the setting within which the group is typically found. The idea of participant observation is that only by immersing yourself in a particular social setting or group can you come to understand the lives of those involved. Participant observation is very similar to, and in many accounts indistinguishable from, the method of ethnography. Some researchers who have used this method have done so *covertly*, that is that they were carrying out the research without the knowledge of the people being studied. A famous example is James Patrick who 'went undercover' to study a delinquent gang in Glasgow (Patrick, 1973). Even when the setting is not an inherently dangerous one as it is in this example, covert research raises serious ethical issues as it violates a fundamental principle of research which is that those involved should give their informed consent to be studied.

So the basic point about qualitative research methods is that they enable the researcher to collect a lot of rich, detailed material about the area being studied. But because it takes time to gather such information this places a limit on the number of people, groups or social settings that can be studied. Qualitative methods using individual cases or small numbers do not enable us to make generalisations to a wider population because we cannot know that they are representative of that wider population. In fact sometimes people or settings are chosen precisely because their peculiarity, or uncommon behaviour, may highlight something we want to focus on.

Unlike quantitative research, qualitative approaches are not concerned with looking for associations between variables or establishing causal relations. They usually produce descriptive accounts of social settings (for example a psychiatric hospital) or the lives of people who have something in common (for example trainee medical doctors). But these accounts will be produced as a result of the researcher's analysis of the interview, observational or other material they have collected. Understanding and analysing this material will involve the development or utilisation of concepts and theoretical ideas in order to help the reader understand what is going on. Students of society can use everyday concepts to analyse their material but sociological concepts and theories are more usefully employed.

An interesting example is to be found in a famous book by Howard Becker called *Outsiders* (1963). In the early 1950s Becker worked as a pianist in the nightclubs of Chicago. This enabled him to undertake a kind of informal participant observation study (although he is not very explicit about the methods of research that he used) of the community of professional musicians that he belonged to.

The first thing we want to draw your attention to is the concept of *community* that we referred to in the last sentence. This again is an everyday concept usually referring to those people living in a particular geographical area. Becker's musicians may well have lived in a certain area but what actually made them a community – what created a sense of belonging of who was an insider and who was an outsider – was their profession and the way in which some aspects of that set them apart from non-musicians. So, again, we have an everyday concept being used in a somewhat different way by students of society. What we commonly think of as a community – those who inhabit a particular neighbourhood – is

122

actually only one instance of a community. When we look closely at what the idea refers to, it is a sense of belonging, of sharing something with others, of having some common interests and maybe a common enemy or two. It is also very much a matter of *identity* (another key concept for students of society but one which we won't go into here). Now geographical location can be one source of these important aspects of our lives but so too can professions or jobs, hobbies, sexual preferences, physical disabilities and many other things.

EXERCISE 15.2

Another widely used concept in the social sciences with a similar meaning to *community* is *subculture*. Find a formal definition of each and think about what the differences are, if any. For this exercise don't use your ordinary dictionary. Instead use a specialist sociology dictionary, an introductory textbook or a social science encyclopaedia.

Another aspect of Becker's analysis that we want to discuss here is the following. These musicians were very able jazz musicians who had high standards in terms of the music that they liked to play. Their self-respect and their standing in the eyes of those who mattered to them – their fellow musicians – depended on playing difficult music well. Unfortunately, however, the music they wanted to play was not a commercial proposition – it didn't bring in much money. So these musicians were forced to play music that they considered beneath them – music that the paying public wanted to listen to – in order to make ends meet. Now in order to show that they held this type of music in contempt and in order to demonstrate that their musicianship should not be judged on the basis of it, Becker's musicians would play such music in an exaggerated way or would insert additional notes or phrases to let their fellow musicians know that they were not taking it seriously. The point about this example is to show how students of society describe certain aspects of group or social life in an analytical way. The musicians that Becker studied were almost certainly aware of this aspect of their behaviour although they probably didn't think about it very much, if at all, and certainly not in the same way as Becker, who was using it to focus on a central element of the culture of the group and one that distinguished the insiders from the outsiders (the audiences and other non-musicians).

Now Becker didn't give a name to this behaviour, but Erving Goffman, another American sociologist, did. He called it 'role distance' and by exploring some of its general features he made the concept more widely available. In order to do this we need to say something about the concept of 'role' which has been a basic (although sometimes controversial) concept within sociology for many years. It is also another concept which we are familiar with in our everyday lives where it can sometimes refer to a kind of job description as in 'what is the role of the teacher'? It also refers to an actor's part in a play or film and it is this usage that Goffman exploits in many of his writings (see especially Goffman, 1959). Sometimes referred to as the dramaturgical perspective (see example below) this approach looks at social life as though we were all playing parts (roles) in a giant play.

THE DRAMATURGICAL PERSPECTIVE

... is an approach that develops the theatrical metaphor to the full, analysing social interaction in terms of performances, scripts, actors, and audiences. Everybody is an actor who has learnt the scripts of various roles which they perform in front of various audiences. The scripts guide our performances rather than determine them. And of course, a social actor is also an audience to the performances of other social actors.

This is not an insight peculiar to modern sociology. The following famous passage comes from Shakespeare's 'As You Like It' (act 2: scene 7),

All the world's a stage,
And all the men and women merely players:
They have their exits and their entrances;
And one man in his time plays many parts,

Like Shakespeare, Goffman also notes that we play many roles and also that the roles we play are taken by others to indicate something about the kind of person we are. Sometimes there are roles, or aspects of roles, that we have to play which we feel may indicate something about us that we are uncomfortable with. In such situations we typically try to 'distance' ourselves from the implications of the role that we are playing. So Becker's jazz musicians were trying to distance themselves from the implications of the popular music that they had to play.

We will discuss all these issues in more detail in the following section when we look at the relationship between theory and research.

In the meantime we will look at the features which distinguish qualitative and quantitative research (see Table 15.1).

> The key features common to all qualitative methods can be seen when they are contrasted with quantitative methods. Most quantitative data techniques are data condensers. They condense data in order to see the big picture. . . . Qualitative methods, by contrast, are best understood as data enhancers. When data are enhanced, it is possible to see key aspects of cases more clearly.
>
> (Ragin (1994) in Neumann (2000: 17))

Whether the researcher uses quantitative or qualitative research methods:

- Their work is a systematic collection and analysis of empirical material.
- They search for patterns which emerge in the data.
- They aim to explain and understand social life.

Table 15.1 Distinguishing quantitative and qualitative research

Quantitative research	Qualitative research
■ Objective facts	■ Social meanings
■ Focuses on variables	■ Focuses on processes
■ Claims to be value-free	■ Values are present and explicit
■ Detached researcher	■ Involved researcher
■ Many cases	■ Few cases
■ Statistical analysis	■ Thematic analysis
Methods employed	*Methods employed*
■ Surveys	■ Observation
■ Interviews – closed questions	■ Interviews – open questions
■ National census	■ Focus groups
■ Government statistics	■ Life-histories
■ Experiments	■ Literature

Adapted from Neumann (2000: 16)

125

TOP TIP

Whenever you read a book, a journal article or another report of a piece of empirical research, look for an account of the methods that were used. Does the author give you enough information to make a decision about whether the research was adequate or not? Try to identify any problems with the research. In particular do you think the findings of the research were influenced by the methods used?

Two mistakes are commonly made when analysing research data. Make sure that you look out for these in other people's work and do not commit them in your own. These are:

1 the ecological fallacy

Do not make assumptions about individual behaviour based on what you know about group behaviour.

As an example: Statistics show that young men between the ages of about 16 and 21 are more likely to commit crime than women of that age. DO NOT assume that all men between those ages have committed a crime.

2 the exception fallacy

Do not make assumptions about group behaviour which are based on what you know about individual behaviour.

As an example: Your (girl)friend is a terrible driver. DO NOT assume that all female drivers are terrible.

So look out for fallacious arguments, poor logic, inappropriate research methods and many other mistakes that can be made by the researcher. And try to ensure that you do not make the same mistakes yourself.

Chapter 16

Linking theory and research

Society is complex, it is made up of a myriad of connections, and also divisions, between people of diverse backgrounds, cultures, nationalities, age groups and so on. People experience society differently depending on their social group, their ethnicity, their class background and their particular interests and ways of engaging in the world. So, if there are many ways to experience the social world, there cannot be only one way to study society – neither can there be one simple way to understand it.

So students of society use different tools in order to:

- study society
- analyse data
- explain different phenomena

In the previous chapter we looked at different methodological approaches which we can use in order to collect data for our research; in this chapter we look at different theoretical approaches we can use to help us *theorise*, or make sense of the world. The word 'theory' can mean many different things across the social sciences and the humanities. In everyday life if we say something is 'theoretical' the implication is usually that the 'reality' is different from, or at least unlikely to accord with, the practice – 'theoretically, we still have a chance of winning the cup but . . .' or 'in theory . . . but in practice'. In the natural sciences 'theory' usually refers to an explanation of something which might or might not be true and efforts are usually directed towards testing it out perhaps by means of an experiment. In the social sciences you will often find reference to 'theoretical perspectives', a phrase which suggests a much broader and looser conception of theory. A perspective is simply a way of looking at something. So you will find that research is often conducted from a particular perspective. This means that the researcher is working with a broad set of ideas but not necessarily a specific set of propositions. These broad theoretical perspectives can mean that the researcher takes different approaches to social research and we explore some of them here.

In Part I we pointed out that research can take many forms. When we refer to *empirical* research we mean research which involves the investigation in some way of people's experiences in the 'real' world. The idea of 'reality' is a tricky one but the notion of a material world that must be attended to in our studies is an integral part of the social sciences. In fact some social scientists have long bemoaned the tendency to produce abstract theory that has no anchorage in concrete phenomena. But it is equally problematic to assume that all that is worthwhile knowing is out there waiting for us to go and pick it up. There is not a simple world of facts where we can find all we want to know. Theory and empirical research go hand in hand. Theoretical ideas can suggest areas of research and guide us in our searches. Our ideas and concepts enable us to develop understandings of the social world that are different from those of 'common sense'.

What is a *concept*?

A concept is simply an abstract idea. Concepts are not peculiar to the social sciences or to science as a whole; they are a feature of our humanity, of the way in which we attempt to make sense of the world. Some social scientific concepts are close to those of everyday life. One example would be that of the 'family'. For many people their families are a significant feature of their lives but they do not usually give much thought to analysing what the concept of 'family' actually refers to. Anthropologists and sociologists, on the other hand, have written a lot of words in an attempt to clarify the key features of a family and they have developed more specific concepts of different types of families such as the 'nuclear' and the 'extended' families. And they have also discussed the relationship of the concept of 'family' to other concepts such as 'marriage' and 'kinship'.

Social scientists don't just *develop* common-sense concepts, however; they may also introduce elements that are just not a part of everyday thinking. Many sociological and anthropological conceptions of the family focus on its utility as a mechanism for social control; for example, how families serve to regulate our actions by placing boundaries on what is considered acceptable behaviour and what would be frowned upon.

EXERCISE 16.1

If you have an introductory sociology textbook take it off the shelf now. If you don't have one, stretch your legs and take a walk to the library and find one. Most, if not all, introductory sociology textbooks have a chapter or section dealing with the family. Look it up and find out what the main features of any two theories of the family are.

Concepts sometimes develop within particular theoretical perspectives; some concepts have a more significant role within some theoretical frameworks than in others; and theoretical perspectives can conceptualise similar phenomena in radically different ways. The concept of 'alienation' for example might be very important to a Marxist considering why young people become involved in breaking the law, whereas a more conservative thinker might find the concept irrelevant to their understanding of crime and offending behaviour.

Some concepts that develop within a social science discipline find their way into everyday, or nearly everyday, language. One example is the concept of 'moral panic'. This was a concept developed within sociology in the late 1960s by two British sociologists, Stan Cohen and Jock Young. It doesn't have as clear a reference point as the family and is harder to pin down. In the box below is Cohen's attempt at a definition.

MORAL PANICS

Societies appear to be subject, every now and then, to periods of moral panic. A condition, episode, person or group of persons emerges to become defined as a threat to societal values and interests; its nature is presented in a stylised and stereotypical fashion ... the moral barricades are manned ...; socially accredited experts pronounce their diagnoses and solutions; ways of coping are evolved or (more often) resorted to; the condition then disappears, submerges or deteriorates and becomes more visible.

(Cohen, 1972: 9)

The concept of moral panic emerged from within a particular theoretical perspective in criminology and the sociology of deviance. This was the perspective known as *labelling theory*. In contrast to many preceding approaches, which had focused on explaining the causes of criminal or deviant behaviour, labelling theory shifted attention to the way in which groups or societies defined and reacted to criminal or deviant behaviour. And, for reasons which we don't have space to go into here, the rationality of defining some particular forms of behaviour as criminal or deviant was called into question. So, for example, before 1967 homosexual behaviour was illegal in Great Britain although there had been a movement to change that for some years. Also in the late 1960s the need to criminalise certain types of drug use, particularly cannabis, was questioned,

The particular form of behaviour that Cohen's research focused on in mid-1960s Britain was a mixture of fighting, rowdiness and vandalism involving groups

129

of young men who came to be depicted as belonging to polarised gangs known as Mods and Rockers. Young's research was on the reaction towards groups of hippies in London's Notting Hill area. In both pieces of research Cohen and Young are clear that they regarded the reactions of the police, the media, politicians and so on to these phenomena as unwarranted by the actual 'threat' that was presented and, in fact, made things worse.

This concept then is one that is contrary to the common-sense understandings of what was going on at the time. The people who 'manned the moral barricades' (to use Cohen's phrase) over the Mods and Rockers or the use of drugs no doubt believed that the threat was a real one and that their behaviour was entirely reasonable.

EXERCISE 16.2

Drug use has often been cited as a focus of many moral panics over the years. Make a list of some other issues which you think have been the subject of moral panics. Look through some current newspapers and watch some television news bulletins. Can you spot some contemporary examples?

Building theories: the importance of research

It is very important for the student of society to learn how to conduct research – whether this be *primary* research or *secondary* research. We have talked about this distinction in previous chapters.

Just to recap: *primary research* helps us to gain knowledge of the world which is currently lacking – we can use *quantitative* research to find out the extent of something, the numbers involved in certain activities, to count the recurrence of certain events and to relate one to another using statistical tools. We can use *qualitative* research to gauge how people feel about certain issues, how they understand the world and what motivates them to make certain life choices.

We can engage in *secondary research* in order to find out what the extent of knowledge already is in an area – what people already know about an issue – then we can categorise and sort this knowledge in various ways in order to help us to make sense of what we already know.

We do research because we have a question that needs answering, so we must:

● Identify the question.
● Identify what is already known about the problem.

130

- Understand the issues which lie behind that question.
- Work towards finding an answer.

Whichever form of research in which we are engaged, research is a disciplined process – there are certain rules which we follow and we take a systematic approach to our research work in order to collect information in as effective and efficient a way as possible.

Research is not just about gathering information, it is also about *analysing* and *interpreting* that information and using it to make predictions or to build theories about the way the world works – or parts of it at least!

ACADEMIC RESEARCH IS *NOT*

- Unanalysed information.

Many organisations collect data, but the academic studies the data and analyses its significance.

- Information collected for its own sake.

The academic collects information for a purpose. One of our ethical codes is that we should not carry out research unless we have a valid and justified reason for doing so.

- Just moving information around from one place to another.

The academic does not merely present existing knowledge to their particular audience, but seeks to further understand and contribute to what is already known.

The importance of theory

As we have pointed out above, there are many different ways of understanding the social world, so we build theories to try to outline the different perspectives which we, or others around us, adopt. It is often said that using theory gives us different '*lenses*' through which we can look to help us to understand what we see. We use theory, then, to help us to understand and to explain what is happening in the world around us. It's a bit like using a microscope lens to see things in close-up detail which we cannot see with the naked eye alone, or using different light wavelengths to look at everyday objects, so that they can appear very different indeed. In the study of society too we can use various theories, or 'lenses' to help us uncover what we cannot otherwise see.

131

It is very important that the student of society learns how to use theory to help them in their various studies, as without theory there is merely personal experience and conjecture or uninterpreted bits of information. Theory gives us the different lenses through which we can interpret our data or attempt an *explanation* of the behaviour of human beings and the social world in general. Furthermore, theory helps us to decide what pieces of information are important and how different 'facts' can be linked and gives us a method by which we can establish the relationship between bits of data.

So theory gives us a particular *perspective* through which we decide what is important and what we are thereby interested in studying. It gives us a range of methods which we will use to carry out that study and gives us a particular lens through which we look which will help us ultimately to analyse and interpret the information we have collected.

The link between theory and research

Sometimes research can be used to generate theory – referred to as *induction*. Sometimes research can be used to test theory – referred to as *deduction*. In the first instance – induction – the research drives the theory-building; in the second instance – deduction – the theory comes first and shapes what the focus of the research will be. You were introduced to the concepts of induction and deduction in the chapter on quantitative methods above. We now explore them in some more detail:

Induction

We do not pluck theories from the air. All theories must be based on systematic inquiry or existing knowledge and understanding. So we base theory on reality – what is actually happening. Without information about the world and the way that it works we cannot build theories which will help us to understand the world and work within it. Some theories are more abstract than others and the more abstract do not engage directly with empirical material or data – but all theories are based on some idea of what the theorist considers to be the 'truth', and the knowledge we use to gauge that 'truthfulness' comes from the material world with which we engage.

Deduction

Without a theory how would you know what ideas were relevant to your enquiry and, left to your own devices without teaching staff to guide you, how would you know what to study? This is where a different theoretical perspective can come in handy. If, like Einstein, you develop a theory that suggests that energy equals mass times the speed of light squared, then you know what to look at, and what to measure in order to test whether your ideas hold up to scrutiny. In the same way when studying society if you are using feminist theory, then you will be likely to focus on the experiences of women and how these may be affected by the dominance of men and male values in society.

However research is used, it plays a key role in the study and understanding of society. Research is not merely the collection of bits of information and a discussion of the methods used to collect them; research involves explaining why data is collected, it involves the interpretation of data and it also involves the formulation of arguments or conclusions which flow from that data and its interpretation.

> So research and theory are intimately related – without theory you would not know what to research and without research you would not be able to build theories to help you to explain the world.

Using theory to work with information

This book is not a simple and straightforward research methods textbook. It does not go through the methods which you can use to collect information or to analyse the data which you do collect. Other books will deal with these issues. However, in the next chapter, we look at how researchers use different theoretical perspectives to guide their research, to collect information and to begin to interpret the data they collect.

Statistical data means very little on its own and has to be understood, interpreted and analysed to help it make sense. In the same way, observations, experiences and events mean nothing on their own; they have to be interpreted and invested with meaning by the researcher.

Take a simple diary of the events which occur in your own life. This might document what you did on different days – where you went, what lectures you should have attended (although you might well have skipped some), who you were meeting that night and where. But this is a very incomplete document and, on its own, says very little about you as a person, about your motivations and lifestyle choices. However, a good researcher might be able to analyse your diary to reveal certain things about you.

A competent researcher might:

- Glean information about you from your diary, such as where you were studying, between which years, what course you took, what work you

133

did, where you tended to hang out socially and how many friends you had.

- Look for patterns in your behaviour, such as how often you attend classes, how you split your life between work and play, whether you always socialise in the same places, with the same people.

At this point a researcher will be beginning to *interpret* the information in front of them and the data which they are using starts to become information – it has started to inform thinking.

You can look at statistics in the same way – tables or columns of raw data mean very little on their own until a researcher peruses them, tracing patterns in the figures and using this to inform their ideas and to build their theories.

Chapter 17

Alternative theoretical approaches

ON PARADIGMS

A paradigm reflects a whole system of thinking, a basic orientation to theory and research.

ON SOCIOLOGY AS A MULTI-PARADIGMATIC SCIENCE

The fact that there is not a single theoretical approach which dominates the whole of sociology might seem to be a sign of weakness in the subject. But this is not so. On the contrary, the jostling of rival theoretical approaches and theories is an expression of the vitality of the sociological enterprise. . . . Human behaviour is complicated and many-sided, and it is very unlikely that a single theoretical perspective could cover all its aspects.

(Giddens, 1997: 578)

As you go about your reading and research you will encounter diverse perspectives. Each perspective has its own philosophical assumptions and principles – its own standpoint as to how society should best be studied.

These perspectives will not necessarily be explicitly declared by the writers and researchers whom you encounter, but the perspective which they take will play an important part in shaping what they write about, how they go about conducting research and which research methods they choose to employ.

Below we outline three of the key approaches which you will encounter in the study of society. These are broad frameworks and within each of these broad perspectives lies a diversity of approaches and theoretical stances; but before you

135

go into more detail you should learn to identify these main approaches to the study of society.

Three key approaches

- positivism
- interpretive social science
- critical social science

Each of these will be described in turn as ideal types. The concept of 'the ideal type' was introduced in Part II, so you will be aware that 'ideal types' are not necessarily found in reality in exactly the way that they are described in theory. 'Ideal types' represent the essential characteristics which lie behind an approach, a methodology or a concept. In reality, different approaches, methods and concepts are more complicated than ideal types would allow and their boundaries may not be so clearly defined. However, each of these definitions of the key approaches used should allow you to identify each as you encounter it. This is important because, in essence, each represents a fundamentally different way of viewing the world – using a different lens.

Positivism

Positivism is the oldest and perhaps most widely used approach to the study of society. You came across its use in the chapter on qualitative research, above. It follows the approach taken by the natural sciences and suggests that there is a world out there which can be observed, recorded and in which these observable phenomenon can be analysed. In other word it employs *the scientific method* which it has borrowed from the natural sciences and applied to the social world. Positivism contends that rigorous and systematic observation of the social world, combined with the application of logic could provide a valuable source of knowledge about the relations of one human to another.

Positivism replaced older ways of seeing the world which depended on more mystical or spiritual explanations for human behaviour and was a revolutionary idea in its time. Students of society no longer had to look for the guiding hand of God or other spiritual forces in order to explain why humans behave the way they do. Positivism is, therefore, an inherently *rational* way of viewing the world – it sees human beings as rational actors who can exhibit some level of choice over how they behave. Prior to the advent of a positivist way of thinking an individual's actions were explained in other ways, for example someone who showed signs of psychiatric disorder, or who broke the law, could be seen as possessed by devils or tried as a witch.

136

The *classical sociologist* Comte is closely linked to the development of this new way of thinking. He actually coined the term 'sociology', but originally used to describe his work as 'social physics', reflecting his view that knowledge of the social world could be produced through the application of scientific methods and principles.

The essential elements of positivism are:

- objectivity
- precise empirical observation
- causality
- prediction

We will go through each of these in turn:

Objectivity

When you take an objective stance towards your work you try to keep some sort of distance from your material. Durkheim suggested that we should study 'social facts as things', that is that those things which we observe going on around us in the outside world should be 'objectified', treated as mere objects to be observed and studied. This means that we step back from any kind of emotional engagement with these 'social facts', we remain steadfastly neutral as observers – like aliens from another planet who observe what is going on in their new surroundings but feel no engagement or attachment to the events or the people under observation. Science is based on what can be seen and recorded – it is not based on values, opinions or beliefs. Only by applying these rules, and strict, logical thinking, can we ensure that as students of society we transcend personal understandings, prejudices and subjective values in order to be able to analyse information in an objective way.

Precise empirical observation

The purpose of positivism is to collect and analyse data in a systematic and detached way in order to discover the 'rules' which govern human behaviour. Positivism is based around the idea that social reality is not made up of random events but that there are patterns to the way we behave which can be discovered through systematic investigation. Of course, human intellect being what it is, these laws are not easily uncovered. The human world is complex, much more so than the natural world, as humans can reason, feel emotions, are influenced by others and live according to social rules and mores. The human world is also riven by divisions and distinctions and each culture and subculture follows its own rules. So positivism stresses the importance of wide-ranging investigations,

137

making numerous observations and measurements and recording the behaviours of as many people as possible.

Causality

Positivism also looks for causal connections between events and behaviours, i.e. it looks at which events might trigger off other events, or how different events might influence the behaviour of individuals. Positivism sees people as driven by self-interest and rationality. Individuals will weigh up the benefits and disadvantages of certain courses of action and will choose that which is most beneficial to them, altering their behaviour in response to outside forces. This happens much the same as any external force acting on a physical object. Once discovered these 'laws' which govern behaviour are said to be 'universally applicable', i.e. they will always trigger the same behaviour in the same circumstances. There is a tendency then for positivism to suggest that human nature is constant, across cultures and different historical time periods – and that the rules that govern behaviour in one place will apply elsewhere – again much like natural laws, such as the law of gravity!

Prediction

Positivism seeks to understand the laws which govern human behaviour in order to predict how changes to our external environment might impact on society. Of course positivism does not assume that people are programmed always to behave in a particular way, but that the consequences of our actions can be estimated – that there is more of a chance that people will react one way rather than another. It is therefore concerned with majority behaviour, rather than that of outliers. Positivism is interested in how people will generally react given a combination of circumstances. So, for positivism, what people do is of more importance than how they might feel when they are doing something.

Identifying a positivist approach

Look for:

- claims or what appears to be a detached, neutral and objective approach;
- measurement of the social world;
- a discussion of causality;
- the use of large data sets;
- the use of statistical analysis.

Research methods used?   *Primarily quantitative*

The interpretive approach

The interpretive approach to studying society is very different from that of positivism. You were introduced to the interpretive approach in the chapter on quantitative research above. This approach can be traced to the work of *Weber*. Weber argued that the social scientist needs to study meaningful social action – that is that we should be interested in behaviour which is carried out with intent and for a purpose. It is not enough to observe what people do but it is necessary to uncover the *social meanings* which drive particular actions. So for the interpretivist, what we do is not so important as *why* we do it. If we understand the motivations behind behaviour, then, the interpretivists argue, we are better able to understand how people are likely to act in different circumstances and how people may react to changes to their environment.

Interpretivists do not look for simple causal connections between events, they acknowledge that complexity in the social world will mean that motivations vary across cultures and across different historical time periods. Interpretivism also seeks to take account of people's emotional reactions to events, their political understandings and the different perspectives which they may bring to an issue or a problem.

The essential elements of interpretivism are:

- observation
- understanding
- interpretation

We will go through each of these in turn:

Observation

Like positivism, interpretivism also relies on observation of the social world in order to gather data – but this is a very different sort of observation from that undertaken by positivists. While positivists observe what happens in the world in order that this can be measured, interpretivists observe the different ways in which people behave in order to understand the meanings which lie behind their actions. In order to do this the interpretivist gets to know a particular setting in some detail. The interpretivist puts themselves in other people's shoes and tries to understand the world from their perspective, seeking to share the feelings and motivations of the people being studied. Under these circumstances the external behaviour which is exhibited, i.e. that which can be easily seen and recorded, is only an indirect indicator of social meaning and in fact can obscure the real meanings behind people's actions. This is because certain actions mean different things for different people, or different things for the same person in different

139

circumstances. So for the interpretivist the simple act of a handshake can signify many different things. A handshake between international heads of government, for example, can be merely a matter of protocol – it might symbolise nothing more than the acknowledgement that a meeting is about to take place. A handshake between two old friends, however, can symbolise warmth and affection and between two political activists might symbolise solidarity and friendship.

Understanding

Interpretivists do not comment on observable behaviour without attempting to understand the meanings which lie behind it. Humans, interpretivists point out, plan their behaviour to a great extent, consider which are acceptable ways of behaving and act accordingly. This is what makes human beings unique in the animal world – we do not act purely on instinct, or for self-gratification. Indeed we can take into consideration the feelings of others and often do. Interpretivists study the very behaviour which makes us unique and seek to understand why someone would do what they do. Interpretivists do not see the action as important but the meanings with which that action is infused. So you might observe thousands of people shaking hands, counting how many men and how many women, and in what circumstances the handshakes took place but without understanding the meaning of the handshake your data would not shed light on this very human contact. Weber called this search for understanding *verstehen*. It involves a great deal of empathy with the subject(s) of the research in order to understand their motivations fully and truthfully. The interpretivist is therefore not a detached observer, far from it; in fact they seek to share the perspective of the researched person or group as fully as possible. The interpretivist will acknowledge the meanings which they place on other people's actions, and in doing so will often expose their own value systems in order to make obvious their own prejudices and distinctions which might get in the way of their understanding of the meanings which other social groups might attribute to the same set of actions. Interpretivists try not to impose their own values onto others but acknowledge that it is difficult not to do so.

Interpretation

Interpretivists seek to interpret actions from the point of view of the person committing the action, and also from the point of view of the person observing the action. We all, knowingly, devise strategies for our behaviour which take into account not only how we interpret our behaviours but how these are socially interpreted – i.e. how other people see them. Take, for example, the very small, but significant, action of the wink. We all, as a matter of course, blink many times a day and this is a purely reflex action to cleanse and moisten our eyes, but if we wink we purposely do something very similar in order to transmit some information to the person to whom we have directed the wink. Again the wink can mean different things to different people in different circumstances, so we have to put ourselves in the place of the winker to try to interpret the individual action, and we have to place ourselves in the role of the person at whom the wink is directed in order to interpret it from their point of view. So interpretivists seek to understand the social rules which govern behaviour in order to interpret and understand the purpose and meaning of human actions. So the interpretivist does not look for universal laws, they acknowledge that meaning may be different for different social actors and that multiple interpretations are possible. Context is very important for the interpretivist because meaning and context cannot be divorced from each other.

Identifying an interpretivist approach

Look for:

- subjectivity;
- relative meanings;
- rich detail and description;
- empathetic understandings;
- context-specific interpretation.

Research methods used?   *Primarily qualitative*

Critical social science

Critical social science is different again from positivism and interpretivism, but it does use elements of both in its methodology. Critical social science is interested in what lies beneath the surface appearance of things. It rejects positivism for being too interested in what is immediately apparent to the observer, and it rejects interpretivism for its relativism, i.e. seeing all points of view as equally valid. Instead critical social science takes a position which states that there are *unequal power relations* in society and that some people hold more power than others. Critical social scientists would certainly argue that there is more than one way of seeing the world, but they would say that certain groups in society control the ideas by which that society is run. Karl Marx, for example, argued that the ideas which are dominant in society are the ideas of the ruling class. In such a situation the ideas which keep one class in power take dominance over all other ideas and perspectives by which others view the world.

Critical social scientists are also concerned to reveal what is hidden in society. They look for the real reason people act in the ways that they do but they acknowledge that people may hide their real motivations or that they may

141

actually not themselves know what motivates them to behave in a particular way. They may take their actions for granted without ever questioning them. *Marx, Habermas, Bourdieu* and *Foucault* are all critical thinkers.

Critical social scientists believe that they must expose the power relations which exist in different social systems and by doing so question the assumptions and ideas which govern the actions we take and the way we live out our lives. It is generally assumed, for example, in current societies across the world that the pursuit of profit is a natural phenomenon, that humans are driven by the desire for material goods and that the profit motive does exactly that – it motivates certain people to get out of bed in the morning and go to work to deliver services or produce goods in order to become rich and be considered successful. However, a critical social scientist might well question this assumption and suggest that it serves the interests of capitalism to make us feel that the only motive for our actions is self-interest and greed. This introduces the concept of 'ideology' – that certain ways of seeing the world come to be seen as fixed and unchanging and more truthful than others. As an example we could look at the profit motive again – the idea that without the motive of profit-making our economic system would collapse, that entrepreneurial spirit would wither away and that no one would be motivated to invent and produce – has become so strongly entrenched in society that it is taken as an absolute truth by many. Critical social science argues that ideology obscures alternative ways of being and thinking. It is therefore up to the critical social scientist to uncover what lies behind certain ideas – and whose interests ideas really serve. This is not an easy thing to do and requires effort and the tool of theory to help reveal the real truth.

Critical social scientists often use *comparative methods* – they compare experiences and ideas across different historical periods, across different cultures and social groups – in order to reveal alternative perspectives. They use such comparisons to demonstrate that there is an alternate way of seeing and experiencing the world and that different people look to alternative sets of ideas by which to motivate their actions. By doing this they question the validity of dominant ideas, then they set out to reveal why certain ideas come to dominate our thinking in the first place.

Critical social scientists often seek to *transform social relations*, to change society for the better. As Karl Marx argued: 'Philosophers have hitherto sought to understand the world in various ways, the point is to change it'.

The essential elements of critical social science:

- looks beyond the surface;
- exposes hidden structures of power;
- uses theory as a tool to expose inequalities;
- realist interpretation;
- action oriented.

142

We will go through each of these in turn:

Looking beyond the surface

Critical social scientists argue that the social world is full of illusions, myths and distortions and that this is how certain groups maintain their power over others. Take the idea of 'race' – some critical social scientists argue that there is no biological basis for the term but that it is socially constructed – that it has become a dominant idea in society because it served a purpose in times of slavery so that slave owners and others could justify the existence of an economic system which kept one set of people dominant over another (see Miles, 1982 for a full explanation of this argument). However, the idea of 'race' has been perpetuated throughout the centuries, even after the abolition of slavery, and critical social scientists try to reveal why the idea of race is still so strong and whose interests this idea serves.

Exposing hidden structures of power

Critical social scientists argue that power structures in society are hidden within most social systems. Today most countries are not run by dictators, who openly flaunt their power over others; instead many countries are considered to be democracies – advanced political systems in which most adults have the right to vote and have their views heard and taken into consideration by politicians. Under such circumstances people can believe that they have a genuine say in how the country is run. Critical social scientists, however, aim to expose political, economic and social inequalities which constrain people's ideas and actions. They point to the fact that although appearances can suggest that 'popular opinion' is sought and incorporated into political decisions, in reality other voices and opinions are considered more powerful and given more weight. When millions of people across the globe marched against the invasion of Iraq in 2003, for example, their views were set aside. Other, more powerful, interests decided that the invasion should go ahead and so it did. The critical social scientist would be intrigued as to why this chain of events came about and whose interests were taken into consideration when the decision was made to invade despite the existence of popular movements which organised against that course of action.

Using theory as a tool to expose inequalities

If the structures of power in society are hidden, then we need a tool to help us to uncover them – theory can be a very effective tool in this regard. Theories help us to regard the world in a different way and by doing so we look

143

for inconsistencies and contradictions which help us to confirm or deny our perspective.

Consider, as an example, the frequently made assumption that women have achieved equality with men in countries such as the United States and Britain of 2005. It is true that, on the surface, it seems that women's lives have changed immeasurably since the development of the women's liberation movement in the 1960s. Women now have the right to hold property in their own name, they can initiate divorce, they are found in many more workplaces, carrying out many varieties of work – both paid and unpaid. The social life of Western women has also altered dramatically; women can be unaccompanied in public space without being considered 'loose', they can express themselves in all sorts of ways – through dress, through the people they choose to date, through the people they choose to spend time with. However, someone using feminist theory to assess the extent of the changes through which women have come in the past 30 years or so would specifically look for evidence to contradict the assumption that women have achieved equality. In doing so they might point to the gender gap in earnings – still around the same level as 30 years ago; they might look to the fact that women are still held mainly responsible for domestic chores and child-care; or they might look to the fear of harassment and assault which many women still experience in public places. So, the use of feminist theory will have alerted them to the fact that everything is not what it seems and that further study needs to take place. The more hidden aspects of women's inequality have thereby been exposed.

So critical social scientists adopt theoretical perspectives which direct their work in particular ways, to specifically look for the contradictions and inconsistencies which will help them gain a deeper understanding of the world.

Realist interpretations of the social world

Critical social science seeks to engage with the realities of people's lives. By doing so, and revealing hidden inconsistencies and power structures, it paints a picture of the world as it really is, rather than how it is assumed that it works. This reduces the power of illusion, myth and ignorance which keeps the real nature of the world hidden from view. Critical social scientists often focus on points of change in society, or points of conflict, as they believe that it is in these times that the balance of society is disturbed, that we can expose the true nature of what lies beneath. It is a bit like an earthquake, or active volcano, which fractures the seemingly so solid surface layer of the planet to reveal the boiling, liquid, turbulent magma on which it actually rests. So critical social scientists focus on contradictions and paradoxes which, when pursued to their source, demonstrate the real nature of the world which we inhabit.

144

In order to truly reveal the realities of the social world critical social scientists often engage in historical and comparative work. By comparing what is in existence today with the way that society operated in other time periods, we can trace changes in our perception and we can assess how much change is apparent or real. Again critical social scientists often compare attitudes and perspectives in different societies in order to break down generally held assumptions – what we take for granted. If, for example, one society accepts that women are as capable as men at owning property and running businesses, and another society does not, then the comparison of these two cultures could expose the false assumptions on which at least one of these must be based (and of course we know exactly which one is false, don't we?).

Orientation on action

Critical social scientists carry out the work which they do, using the perspective which they use, because they are concerned about inequalities. By revealing the inconsistencies and contradictions in the way society is run they therefore hope to make some sort of difference – either to inform those with the power and ability to change things, or to call people to action. By exposing the ways in which women are still constrained and subject to discrimination, for example, it would be hoped that women themselves can attempt to counter this, and/or that people in charge of making decisions in areas which inhibit women's progress will be more aware of the impact of their decisions and will act accordingly, to reduce negative consequences of their actions.

So critical social scientists, in common with positivists and unlike interpretivists, believe that there is a reality out there which *can* be exposed. Unlike positivists, however, they do not see this reality as universal and unchanging, but they believe that that it alters frequently and that it can also be changed by the action of humans.

Identifying a critical social science approach

- the author will often state their own perspective and values;
- a particular theoretical standpoint is often articulated;
- historical-comparative work is used;
- a political bias may be assumed or is stated;
- the work is action oriented and can be written for or disseminated to non-academic audiences.

Research methods used?   *Either qualitative or quantitative, but always with a critical stance.*

145

Using theory to reflect on society

> Sociology is the study of human social life, groups and societies. It is a dazzling and compelling enterprise, as its subject matter is our own behaviour as social beings. The scope of sociological study is extremely wide, ranging from the analysis of passing encounters in the street to the investigation of global social processes.
>
> (Giddens, 1997: 2)

As this quote from Giddens demonstrates, the study of society can take place at many different levels, from the micro level – the minutiae of day-to-day life – to the macro level – up to the level of decisions and actions which take place at a global level. Where you choose to focus along this continuum is ultimately up to you; however, whatever you choose to study, the use of theory will help you to see the object of your study in different ways. Again, according to Giddens, sociological theory 'transforms the meaning and power of everyday knowledge' and allows us 'to think ourselves away from the familiar routines of our daily lives in order to look at them anew' (1997: 3).

This last point by Giddens presents the key to studying society as a sociologist rather than just as an interested observer, such as a journalist might be said to be. In Part I we introduced Wright Mills' idea of 'the sociological imagination'. Cultivating such an imagination helps you to place whatever you study in a fully social context, so that you develop the tools to understand your own experiences from different perspectives, and to begin to understand the experiences of others. Once you start to explore your own and other people's experiences from these different perspectives you should begin to see the world anew.

Many questions have stretched the minds of sociologists. Some of the key debates are set out below:

■ To what extent does society constrain or limit our behaviour?
■ How do certain social practices become acceptable?
■ What control do individuals have over their lives?
■ How does change come about?
■ Is consensus more important than conflict?

Can you even begin to answer all these questions without the aid of sociological theory?

146

When you start to study society it is tempting to bring all your old assumptions, prejudices and former ways of thinking to the subjects you are studying. Try not to do this. Try to open up your mind to the different perspectives which you will encounter in your studies. Don't dismiss these ideas if they differ from your own; instead, try them out and see if they fit – see if they help to shed light on issues and problems – if they do then they are worth considering.

EXERCISE 17.1

Think about your own views and begin to question them. Ask yourself:

- Where do my ideas come from?
- How strongly do I hold them?
- Are they adequately formulated?
- What evidence informs them?
- Would I rethink them, given new evidence?

Now use these questions to interrogate the views of every other person you come across in the course of your study, whether these be other students or major theorists.

If you use theory effectively you should find that the way you look at things should alter significantly – if, for example, at the end of three years' study you think exactly the same way about the world that you did when you started, you have probably been doing something wrong! If, however, you have started to think about the world in different ways, then you should find your studies both exciting and rewarding.

Diversity in theoretical thinking provides a rich source of ideas that can be drawn on in research, and stimulates the imaginative capacities so essential to progress in sociological work.

(Giddens 1997: 578)

Part V

Communicating your ideas

THE IMPORTANCE OF COMMUNICATION

There is little point in collecting data, developing a critical eye and adding to knowledge or understanding of a subject if the student of society keeps all this to themselves. For this reason we write books, journal articles, contribute papers to seminars and conferences and conduct book reviews, and students write essays and are asked to present at seminars in order to develop their communication skills. Communicating clearly is an important skill, but many students find it hard to translate what they have learned into the written or spoken word. This chapter gives you some tips as to how to communicate your ideas to others in a way that makes most sense to the reader or listener and leaves them with little doubt as to your overall argument. Also, pulling your thoughts together to communicate them to others is helpful in deepening your own understanding of the material.

How to write essays, dissertations and reports, give presentations and communicate over the Internet are all covered in more detail in later chapters. First we set out some basic ground rules for all types of communication.

Prepare for an intelligent, yet ill-informed layperson

When you are putting your thoughts together it is a good idea to think of your audience as an intelligent, but ill-informed layperson. This means that you are not writing for an expert so you will have to patiently explain your position, presenting the evidence which informs your argument and supporting every point you make by citing relevant sources – whether this be of theory or data.

Construct an argument

Don't just list relevant facts or theoretical perspectives. It is important to weave an argument throughout your written work or presentation. And remember to direct this argument towards the question which you have set out to answer. Your points should flow in a logical sequence, and you should be able to link the different points which you make; perhaps one point will follow on from another, or will contradict a previous point – let your reader or listener know that you are aware of this and why you are presenting these points in your work.

Structure your written work or presentation

It is surprising how many students submit written work or give presentations that are not properly structured. Your work or presentation must have:

- an introductory section which explains what you are going to do;
- the body of work or presentation, in which you do what you said you would do;
- a conclusion in which you bring the different strands of your argument together and summarise what it is that you have learned from the material.

Never introduce new material into your conclusion.

Consider alternative explanations

Make sure that you look at the issue from more than one standpoint. Explain what each perspective brings to the study, how they differ and if each sheds a different light on the problem. Remember, there is always more than one way to look at an issue, and even if you are asked to look at one theoretical standpoint and its contribution to an issue you will only be able to do this effectively if you contrast this standpoint with other ways of looking at the problem.

Cite your sources

It is very important to acknowledge where you obtained your information or your ideas. See Chapter 24 in this book on Referencing to see how important this is and how you can make sure that you cite other people's work in your own.

Read through your work and check it thoroughly

Always read through your work or presentation notes to check that they make sense, that you have done what you set out to do and that you have been clear and concise. Use the following ways of checking your work to ensure that it is well presented:

- Use the spell check facility – most work you present will be produced on a computer using word-processing software. Make sure this is switched on when you write and check spelling in your dictionary as you go along. Make sure that you have the correct spell check on for the country in which you are writing. However,

150

spell-checking software is not infallible, so you will need to go through your work yourself. Spell checks will not include many difficult theoretical terms, nor will they be able to spell the names of authors. Spell-checking software will also not alert you to a wrongly spelled 'hear' or 'here', 'their' or 'there' and other words which are very similar – so these will have to be checked manually.

- Look for grammatical mistakes. Word processing software also has functions for checking grammar, but these are often crude and more trouble than they are worth, so make sure you read your work very thoroughly to check the grammar. It is often a good idea to read your work out aloud when checking grammar, ideally to someone else, so you can check that the way you have structured your sentences conveys the sense which you intended.

- Check that your argument flows logically throughout. Have you made the links between each point? Does one point lead to another, or do some points contradict each other? Have you made this clear to the reader or listener?

- Check your paragraphing. A paragraph should contain and elucidate one point. If a piece includes lots of short paragraphs it probably means that each point has not been sufficiently dealt with or explained. If the paragraphs are too long – i.e. more than about half a page in length, then they probably contain too many points – or show that you have digressed into a waffly sort of style.

- Check that the work is well structured. Read the conclusion, then your introduction – have you done what you said you would do? Does your conclusion accurately summarise your argument?

151

Chapter 18

Writing essays

One of the main ways in which people ensure that their ideas can circulate in the public domain is through publishing their work in books and journals. Despite the rise in other forms of communication such as websites, email and film, the published and written word is still a very valued way in which to transmit ideas to as wide an audience as possible. Books are still an extremely flexible method by which to exchange ideas and to keep a permanent record of the development of arguments and different ways of thinking. Websites can disappear from the Internet or move their location, emails are less permanent and more private forms of communication, and films need television, cinema or video-players to watch and are still quite difficult to flick through to the most relevant parts. Books and journals, however, are stored in libraries, are easy to retrieve and are still incredibly flexible to use. It is therefore very important for students to develop the art of writing and ensuring that they can convey their ideas as clearly as possible using the written word.

Why write essays?

Writing essays as a student can often seem a strange and unnatural thing to do. After all, unless you pursue an academic career it is rare that you will write essays at any other time of your life. However, there are many reasons for essay writing, and many of the skills which you use when constructing an essay will be useful to you at other times. In the current jargon, learning to write essays will mean that you develop 'transferable skills' which will be useful to future employers and which you might also use in other areas of your life. Consider the following:

- Awareness of current thinking in a subject area.
- Working with relevant information.
- Constructing an argument.
- Making points clearly and concisely.

- Weighing up evidence.
- Drawing logical conclusions.

You can see that each of these is a useful skill to acquire in itself, but all are essential to good essay writing.

TOP TIP: ESSAY GRADING

There is another good reason for learning to write essays. Much of your course-work will be assessed in this way.

Improving your essays may not involve a lot more work. Essays are likely to receive higher marks and perhaps even a higher class if you are able to demonstrate to your examiner that you have acquired all of the skills listed in the bullet points above.

So if you are interested in getting better marks, read on!

Planning the essay

It is important to plan your essay carefully. People plan their essays in many different ways – sometimes they 'brainstorm' and write everything down that they know about the topic and then copy and paste the most relevant ideas into the body of the essay. Some make lists of important ideas or information and then try to make links between them. Others first construct diagrams with links from one idea to another to make sure that different points connect. Whichever you choose you must make sure that your work has a structure or framework and that the various parts and paragraphs of the essay relate to each other.

- Introduction – say what you intend to do.
- Review of the literature – see section on Literature Reviews below.
- Present the argument and points to consider.
- Conclusion – summarise what you have done.

TOP TIP

There are usually several positions from which to approach any essay topic. Make sure you know what they are and work them into your essay in a clear way. Often other areas covered in a module can be used to throw some light on the topic of your essay.

Writing essays: step one

Reviewing the literature and working with relevant information

You will need to start any piece of work by researching what is already known about the particular subject in which you are interested. You do this by allocating the early part of your essay to a review of the existing literature.

WHAT IS A LITERATURE REVIEW?

A literature review is *an examination/analysis of accumulated knowledge about a particular question.*

In a literature review you will:

- Summarise what is known about a subject.
- Demonstrate that you understand what you have read.
- Outline different perspectives.
- Show how thinking has developed in a particular area.

Summarising what is known about a subject

It is generally advisable to find out what is already known about a question before you begin to answer it yourself. In this way you will avoid 're-inventing the wheel' and wasting valuable research time. When you begin *your own* research, conducting interviews and surveys with real research subjects, this exercise will become vital. All researchers should take great pains to ensure that they are not inadvertently recreating work which has already been carried out by someone else. We research and write in order to build on existing knowledge and to understand our subject more fully; we do not carry out research just for the sake of creating work for ourselves or others. This is an important issue to consider when writing essays. You should ask yourself how you can use existing work to help you to understand a subject and to answer the question posed.

Of course you can never know all that there is to know about a particular subject, but you must demonstrate in your work that you are aware of the main arguments/theories/facts which relate to your essay topic. Earlier sections of this book have already outlined how to go about searching for information in a particular area, so you should use these techniques to collect the reading which you are going to use to answer the question which you have been set.

155

TOP TIP

Read widely and do not base your writing on a limited number of sources. Be especially careful not to rely on textbooks alone when constructing your essays.

When you have collected all your information together you need to *summarise* the main points which are made in the literature you have read. This will include a discussion of relevant:

- theories
- research
- data

Looking at theoretical arguments will point you to the key ways in which you can tackle the essay. However, it is often a good idea to illustrate your argument with 'real world' examples. Examining different research studies and other data in the area of your writing can cast light on a particular problem and demonstrate how different theoretical positions might relate to what happens 'in the 'real world'.

Demonstrating that you understand what you have read

Summarising the main points made by an author can be a difficult exercise. You must decide which are the key points that the author is making. Remember that you only have a limited number of words to work with. Make sure that your work is concise and focused. You do not need to discuss *all* the points raised by your reading, but you will need to discuss the *main* points which shed light on the question you have been set. If you can successfully outline which points are most relevant to your essay you will demonstrate that you are able to understand what you are reading. If you include arguments which are irrelevant to your topic, or are perhaps only marginally useful, the reader will believe that you do not really understand the question you have been set, or have misunderstood the main points which you have read and this may well affect the marks that you receive. Look closely at the work and outline:

- the main points that the author is making;
- the evidence which the author uses to make these points;
- if possible, the theoretical position the author adopts.

TOP TIP

Sometimes authors will outline the theories which they are using in their writing in their introductory comments and also usefully summarise the points they have made in their concluding comments. Read the introduction and conclusion first to help you to understand where the author intends to go with their arguments.

Make sure that you use your own words when summarising the work of other writers. Do not try to force your writing into an 'academic' style. Use a style of writing that you are comfortable with. Your writing will be much clearer as a result.

TOP TIP: 'TO QUOTE OR NOT TO QUOTE'

Do not use too many quotes. Only use a quote when it helps to illustrate a point that you have already made. Never use a quote instead of attempting an explanation of the point in your own words. This indicates to the reader that you may not really understand what you have read.

Outlining different perspectives

As a student you soon discover that there is more than one way of addressing any issue. In Part IV we explored how academics use different theoretical positions when exploring a particular issue. Sometimes writers will disagree with the theoretical standpoint of others, or will disagree with either the way in which another writer has interpreted their data or with the logic of their argument. In the social sciences there is rarely only one accepted way of exploring or understanding an issue. Try to explain how, and why, each perspective differs and if there are any similarities between the approaches.

Many essay questions require the student to discuss different ways of addressing their subject. Some will clearly state that this is what is needed, many will not; however even an essay question which asks for an exploration of one particular perspective will benefit from your taking up a critical position towards the end of the essay. This will mean a discussion of some of the shortcomings of the perspective and will involve some analysis of alternative ways of looking at the question.

Showing how thinking has developed in a particular area

Academics learn from each other's work and build upon the work of others. Try to show how the work which you have read has been influenced by other authors. Sometimes an author will come up with a new perspective on an issue which sheds a completely different light on the subject and results in a new way of looking at the issues. However, academics are influenced by, and build upon, the work of others, so these 'paradigm shifts' in thinking do not come out of the blue. Look at whether there have been any major shifts in thinking about the topic which you are studying. When did these arise and why might they have happened?

TOP TIP

By the second or the third year of your undergraduate degree you should be linking up what you have learned in the different modules which you have taken across your degree course.

Think about what you have studied in your theory courses which might help you to understand more substantive issues.

Think, also, about how the different substantive topics which you have studied might relate to one another or to other topics. The best work demonstrates these links.

Writing essays: step two

Constructing an argument and making points clearly

Now you have constructed your literature review. However, academic essays usually require more than just a presentation of what is known in an area. You will now have to use the information you have collected to address a particular question and attempt to answer it. In order to address your specific question you will need to develop an argument which leads to a particular conclusion. You will need to convince the reader that you have come to a valid conclusion by presenting a reasoned and logical argument, backed up by evidence which is based on a good range of sources.

The main body of your essay should consist of your argument, which is clearly presented, logically argued and supported by relevant reading, examples and evidence.

Addressing the question

The first stage of writing an essay is to understand the question that you have been set. Look at the essay title carefully. What is it asking you to do? You *must* address the issue as the essay title or question suggests.

Below are some key words which may appear in the essay title and which should alert you to what you must do in the essay:

- *Describe*   To give a detailed account of something.
- *Outline*   To set out the key components of the theory/issue/activity.
- *Discuss*   To go beyond description to explore in detail.
- *Consider*   To look at something from more than one perspective. To assess the value of each perspective.
- *Compare*   To examine similarities and differences between different perspectives.
- *Contrast*   To weigh up the advantages and disadvantages of each.
- *Evaluate/ appraise*   To describe and consider the advantages or problems associated with a theory/activity.
- *Illustrate*   To use examples to clarify an issue.
- *Demonstrate*   To use examples to prove an argument to be correct/incorrect.
- *Examine*   To question the evidence related to a particular issue or standpoint.
- *Explore*   To fully investigate a claim.
- *Summarise*   To give a concise account of the key components of an idea.

Making your points clearly

Write clearly using your own words. Remember, the main aim is to *communi-cate* your ideas. You should assume that the reader is an intelligent but naive person, that is that they know little about the subject but that they will question your assumptions and you have to work to convince them of your argument.

Here are a few tips to help you to perfect your writing style:

- Write in clear and focused sentences. If a sentence is too long then break it down into two or more sentences, each dealing with a separate point.
- Make sure that each point follows from the next and that you cover all aspects of the argument.
- If you move to a different point, then start another paragraph. If your paragraphs are too short, you are probably not taking enough time on each point.

159

- Read through your work. Does it make sense? Does the argument flow? Ask someone else to read it and comment if you are not sure.
- Draft and redraft each piece of work. It is rare that anyone writes perfectly on a first draft.

Writing essays: step three

Presenting evidence to support your points

It is essential that every major point which you make in your work is backed up by some kind of evidence or data. It is surprising how many times students submit work which may have some very valid points and interesting discussions but which fails to produce any evidence which supports the arguments made. In the age of the Internet, where a great deal of information is available to us all without even leaving our computer screens, this is inexcusable! In Part II and on our website we cover some of the best sources of information available to the student of society, and in Part III we looked at how students can ensure that the sources of information which they use are valid and reliable, so we will not go over this again here.

There are various sources of evidence which you can use in your work:

- Primary data – this is information which you would collect yourself, for example through the use of questionnaires or interviews.
- Secondary data – this is data which has already been collected by other researchers. This could be in the form of statistics or other forms of research such as focus groups, analysis of images or texts or interviews.
- Citing the work of others.

If you do not support your points with some kind of evidence, then this signals to the reader that:

- you may be relying on hearsay;
- you have not looked for evidence;
- you have not found any evidence;
- there is no evidence to back up your idea.

This would signal that your work is not rigorous and/or well informed and such work is not a valid way for the academic to present arguments.

160

Writing essays: step four

Weighing up the evidence

Because the social sciences deal with issues that relate to our own lives/societies, you will already have some knowledge of the topics you write about gleaned from television, newspapers, talking to friends, personal experiences and so on. You may not even be aware of some of this knowledge; much of what we know we just take for granted most of the time. Or you may have developed strong opinions about some of the issues and problems in our society or the world today. This knowledge and these opinions are not necessarily ill-informed, but you still need to question them. Before you start on an essay you should sit down and work out what is your starting position; what do you already know about the topic; what do you think about the issues involved?

You must then reinforce your knowledge with more reading. Do not choose your sources because they reinforce your own views or reject those that do not. Consider perspectives other than your own. What do other people think about the issues, and how does this differ from your own views? What evidence can you present to support your views and what evidence do others present to support theirs? Try to be even-handed about opinions and knowledge which goes against your preconceptions. Perhaps you need to modify your views in the face of this evidence or perhaps the evidence to support your views is strong. Take your reader through the logical sequences of your argument and explain why you prefer one piece of evidence over another.

Here are a few tips to help you weigh up the evidence accurately:

- Do not make a statement without ensuring that it is supported by some evidence or, if you have read this in the literature, that the source is accurately referenced.
- Remember that there is little if anything in the social sciences that holds true in all situations at all times, so be cautious in what you say. Use phrases like 'according to research carried out by Smith (1987) . . .' or 'according to the research of Jones (1988) it appears that . . .' rather than merely stating that something is true.
- Avoid wild generalisations. Don't write 'men are more criminal than women'; instead write something along the lines of 'according to official statistics (Home Office, 1996) men are more likely than women to be convicted of a criminal offence'.
- Do not use phrases such as 'research shows that . . .' This is meaningless unless you can refer to the actual research you have in mind.
- Do not use phrases such as 'it is well known that . . .' How do you know what is 'well known' and why should 'well known' be a recommendation? It could still be wrong!

161

Concluding your essay

Conclusions are used to focus the reader onto the main points that you have made in your work. Never introduce new material in your conclusion. Use the conclusion to summarise, but not to repeat, your argument. If you have been asked to do more than describe a problem you can also use the conclusion to make your own views known, although you should avoid this in the main body of the essay.

Chapter 19

Writing dissertations

Many degree courses in the social sciences require students to write a dissertation in their final year. The mark you get for your dissertation can have a big effect on the class of your degree. This is because it is will usually account for a quarter or a third of your final-year marks which will probably carry a greater weight than your marks from previous years. Much of what we have said about writing essays also applies to dissertations but there are some additional comments and tips that we cover in this section.

What is a dissertation?

A dissertation is an extended piece of work on a topic of your own choice, typically around 10,000–12,000 words long. Preparing a dissertation enables you to develop your knowledge of a particular topic to a much greater depth than is possible in taught courses and also develops your ability to work independently, to plan your work and to marshal, analyse and present large amounts of material.

In assessing the dissertation the markers will be concentrating on your ability to integrate different aspects of your studies and to build on knowledge which you have already acquired throughout your degree course. They will also be looking for you to demonstrate your skills in the gathering and managing of a considerable amount of information and that you can use this information to produce an extended, coherent argument on your particular topic.

As ever, the precise expectations with regard to a dissertation will vary from university to university, so you should check that you are fully aware of what rules apply to you.

The dissertation may be based primarily on secondary material, e.g. books, articles, official statistics, etc. or it may involve a small piece of empirical research.

Whilst the emphasis is on you working independently, you will be allocated a supervisor who will help to guide your studies.

Choosing the topic of the dissertation

Although you are likely to have a fair degree of choice in the topic to be covered by the dissertation, it will probably have to be approved by your supervisor. This is done for your own protection – to make sure you have a viable project which will give you a chance to demonstrate your abilities to best effect.

As we have already said, choosing a topic to research or a question to ask can be very difficult. Most students initially have only a very broad idea of what they wish to cover in their dissertation. This then has to be narrowed down after an initial period of reading on the subject. Your supervisor can help you to focus your reading and help you to 'narrow down' your focus to something which will make a decent dissertation.

It is a good idea to choose a topic which is linked in some way to one or more of the modules that you have already taken or that you will take alongside the dissertation in your final year. This will help to ensure that your dissertation is grounded in, and informed by, a relevant body of knowledge.

Look over reading lists and lecture outlines from modules you have taken or look at some books relating to the general area that you are interested in (crime, sex, work or whatever). Think about previous essays you have done; it is usually OK to take a topic that you have already written an essay on and develop it further in a dissertation, but obviously you can't recycle the essay. Think about essay topics you didn't choose to do; are there any that you were interested in but didn't do at the time for some reason? You could of course just focus on a part of an essay and develop that.

What to expect from your supervisor

You may meet your supervisor individually, as part of a group, or, most probably, a mixture of both. These days many supervisors and students conduct a lot of their business by means of email. Your supervisor will provide help and guidance in preparing your dissertation but you must recognise that you will be mainly working independently and must accept the responsibility to plan your work, police your interim deadlines, prepare drafts and so on.

Check what applies at your institution, but the following are some of the typical roles of the supervisor:

- Initial discussions to help you focus on a topic for your dissertation.
- Helping you to identify suitable sources.
- If necessary, discussion of which modules should be taken in association with the dissertation.
- Providing some guidelines as to how to 'break up' a dissertation into linked chapters.
- Helping you to identify tasks and to set deadlines.

- Regular meetings to discuss the progress of your work.
- Commenting on drafts *provided they are submitted well in advance of the deadline*

Your supervisor cannot be expected to organise you. That is your job; you must make sure that you attend arranged meetings and complete work targets by the agreed deadlines. You can't expect your supervisor to be available to provide help if you leave things until the last minute.

Working on your dissertation

A dissertation of 10,000–12,000 words may seem a lot but if you think about it as the equivalent of $4 \times 2,500$–3,000 word essays, it doesn't seem so daunting. Again there may be local rules that apply to you but typically a dissertation will consist of three or four main chapters of about 2,500–3,000 words each sandwiched between an introduction and a conclusion. There is nothing set in stone about the number of chapters – some dissertations have more, but unless your supervisor tells you otherwise, we would suggest you go for at least three chapters and no more than five. The important thing is to think about ways to break up your topic into several areas which will link together.

You may be surprised to find that you are expected to begin work on your final year dissertation before you have even finished your second year. At the very least you will be expected to come up with a general topic area so that you can be allocated to a supervisor. You will also probably be expected to meet your supervisor before the end of the year to discuss it with them.

You might (quite rightly) think that you deserve a holiday and you don't want to be spending time on academic work over the summer holidays. But there are several things that you can be doing which aren't too taxing and which can make a big difference so that you 'hit the ground running' in the autumn.

What to do over the summer!

Think

You can think about your topic wherever you are. You can do this whilst you are lying on the beach or stacking shelves in a supermarket, watching television or whatever you will be doing over the summer. As soon as you can, though, write your thoughts down.

Set up a file

Get a physical folder labelled Dissertation and put six folders inside labelled, Introduction, Chapter 1, Chapter 2, Chapter 3, Conclusion, Bibliography. Do the same on your computer. It doesn't matter if you don't know what your chapters are going to be about yet. Think about these folders as receptacles which you will gradually fill up with material over the year.

Check what material you have already

There should be some things you have covered on modules in your first and second years which relate to your dissertation. So dig out any relevant lecture and other notes and put them in your folders. Think broadly – so, for example, if your topic is a particular type of crime, anything you have got on criminological theory is likely to be of some use.

Start to compile a list of sources

A good place to begin is to look at the reading lists of any relevant modules that you have taken. Make a list of any sources that look as though they might be useful. *Make sure you keep full details of any sources in your computer and other files.* You will build up quite a large bibliography (probably around 30 items or so) and you don't want to be rushing around in March trying to track down some of the details.

Keep an eye on the media

Although the use of media material can be problematic, it is useful for you to read any newspaper articles or watch any television programmes relevant to your topic. Make sure you keep a note of all the details. You can often find interesting examples that you can use to illustrate your dissertation and give it an 'up-to-date' feel.

Read

Your reading doesn't have to be only of academic sources; no one expects you to take academic tomes away on holiday with you, but look out for novels, auto/biographies and other popular works that relate to your topic – they may not end up in your bibliography but they can be helpful in stimulating new ideas.

Start writing

It is never too soon to begin writing. It is best to write a little bit regularly even if it is rubbish – you can always throw it out later.

Facts and figures

Many (but not all) dissertations will need to include or refer to some 'facts and figures' – some basic empirical data relating to the topic. So, for example, if you are writing about a particular form of crime, you will need to know things like what the law actually says about it, how much of it there is and what do we know about the perpetrators. So start collecting this kind of information – much of it may well be available online at government department websites for example. This is something you can do when you are not feeling too creative.

General tips for completing a successful dissertation

- You should get organised and plan ahead. You can't rely on a particular book being available just when you want it, so you may need to put in an order for it at your library. Some relevant books and journals may not be available in your local library but you may be able to order them through an inter-library loan scheme if you leave yourself enough time.
- No one writes perfectly in a single draft. Expect to redraft your work several times to make it readable/clear/grammatical/interesting and well structured. Find some friends who are willing to read your work and be constructively critical about it.
- Write clearly. This is a good general rule anyway but whoever marks your dissertation will have a lot of others to mark and only a limited time in which to do it. They won't waste time trying to figure out what you mean if it is not obviously clear.
- In your introduction tell your reader what they can expect to find in the following chapters. It will help them if they have an idea of what your plan is.
- Try to think of an interesting title for the dissertation. 'A Sociological Study of Unemployment' may be an accurate description of the content but it is not very attractive. 'No Work To Go To: a Sociological Study of Unemployment' retains the descriptive phrase but is a more attractive proposition for your reader.
- Also try to think up some attractive, and descriptive, titles for your chapters rather than just leaving them as Chapter 1, Chapter 2, etc.

Presentation of dissertations

This is something else that will vary from university to university or department to department. Make sure you check out what applies to *you*. Unless they are contradicted by your local rules the following are some suggestions we have:

- To make it easy for the markers to read use double spacing and a clear font such as Times New Roman or Arial with a point size of no less than 12.
- Number the pages. You can possibly get away with not doing this in an essay but a dissertation of 10,000 words will take up probably at least 30–40 pages, so they must be numbered.
- Preliminaries. These are the pages that come before the main material. There should be a title page which includes your name, the degree for which you are registered, the title of the dissertation and the date submitted. This should be followed by a page containing a list of the contents of the dissertation and the page number at which each part begins. The preliminary pages will then be followed by your main chapters, any appendices, and the bibliography.
- Check whether you are required to have your dissertation bound. Even if this is not compulsory it is a good idea and can be done inexpensively, but you should certainly make sure that the pages of your dissertation are secure and that it will not fall apart as it is read.

Chapter 20

Writing reports

More and more students are being asked to work with outside organisations and conduct research with them, or reflect on their experiences of an organisation. You may well be required to do this in the course of your own study, and then to write a report on some aspect of your work.

Reports differ from essays or dissertations. In essay writing you are required to use the information which you have collected to answer a particular question and/or to construct a coherent and logical argument. This is not the function of a report. If you are asked to write a report you must first and foremost *report* what is known about a particular subject, then report what you have to add to that knowledge. You will then analyse and assess the information which you have included in the report in order to make some recommendations or to draw out some key conclusions for the reader.

WRITING IN SECTIONS

As the function of a report is different from that of an essay, reports are constructed differently.

Essays are constructed around an argument which flows throughout the piece, as such they are written in a style which reflects this. They are rarely 'broken up' into chunks or sections as each point must relate to the last, or to previous lines of reasoning. Essays should not usually include bullet points or lists, for the same reason. Reports, however, are *typically* 'broken up' into sections. This demonstrates to the reader that the author has finished writing about one aspect of the subject and is about to move on to another. Bullet points, lists, text boxes and the use of relevant headings or subheadings are also common in reports.

This division of reports into separate sections helps make the report easier to read. Reports will present the reader with a lot of information and it helps to present information in sections in order to draw the reader to particular points which they might find most useful.

Consider the way that this book is laid out. It is designed so that the reader will be able to find those sections which are most relevant to them as easily as possible. The use of different fonts, icons, shaded areas, tables and diagrams all help to break up a lot of information into more easily readable chunks. If each section was written in one long piece, without boxes and highlighted sections, it would be much more difficult to use. Think of this when constructing your own reports.

Writing reports: step one

Planning the report

Reports include a lot of information, so you need to be clear about where to place the information which you are presenting.

- Set out why and by whom the report has been commissioned.
- Present the issue which the report is meant to address.
- Present what is known about the issue.
- Present your own findings (if you have collected your own data).
- Discuss the data.
- Make recommendations to your reader.
- Provide an 'executive summary' or 'key findings'. These are often placed at the beginning of the report for ease of access.
- Place any additional information in different Appendices at the end of the report.

Plan the report carefully, make sure that you are placing your information, your analysis and your recommendations into the appropriate sections and try not to mix these up together.

Use the website to link to various reports to see examples of how different reports are set out.

Writing reports: step two

Constructing the different sections

The title page

Reports should have a title page. This should include:

- the name of the report
- the author of the report (this may be an individual or an organisation)
- details of who commissioned the report
- the date the report was presented to the commissioning body

The list of contents

Include a list of contents, with page numbers, after your title page. This will help the reader identify exactly which sections are most relevant to them. They may want to skip the detail and start by looking at your analysis, or your recommendations – or they may be searching for a particular piece of data and your list of contents should enable them to do this quickly and accurately.

TOP TIP

Most word-processing software can generate a table of contents for you. To do this you must use the appropriate Headings and Sub-headings functions on your word-processing package. Then, if you change any sections around, the word processor can update the Table of Contents for you. This is especially useful if you are writing long, complicated reports.

The introduction

The reason for the report should be included here. What problem(s) does the report set out to address? Perhaps you have been given a brief for the report. If so you should make sure that your introductory comments outline the brief and explain how you set about answering the brief.

Existing data or knowledge

In this section you should set out what is already known about the subject which you are to address. This is similar to the literature review which you would construct for an essay, but is likely to include a more detailed presentation of data rather than theory. You should look at different aspects of the subject. As with the literature review, you should look at the subject from different angles, presenting the different practical and theoretical positions which have been utilised to look at this subject in the past. Examine their strengths and weaknesses and what each has to offer to a possible solution to the subject under scrutiny.

Adding to existing data or knowledge

Use this section to present your own data, if you have conducted your own research, or to add your own perspective to the data which you have already presented.

Some more technical information can be placed in an Appendix at the end of the report.

A TECHNICAL APPENDIX COULD INCLUDE:

■ the methods which you used to obtain the data;
■ the sample of people whom you chose to collect the data from;
■ any problems which you encountered and how you overcame these;
■ any ethical issues which arose in the course of your research.

Your data need to be presented in as clear a way as possible. Avoid using long descriptive paragraphs and instead use tables, diagrams or pictures to demonstrate what the data show and to illustrate your points. For hints on how to use these most effectively see below.

If you have not conducted your own research then this section might include a discussion of how your report has helped to throw a new light on the problem by bringing all the information which you have used together.

All researchers find that they will not need to present every single finding which they have uncovered. It is important to assess which of your findings are relevant to the question or issue on which you have been asked to report, and to focus on these, relevant, areas of your data.

Discussing the data

After you have presented all the data, you need to discuss what you have presented. In this section you should look at:

- How the information which you have presented relates to the original brief of the report?
- How it may help to shed light on the issue?
- How it may be interpreted in different ways?
- What might be missing from the data?

The discussion is separated from the presentation of the data so that the reader can interpret the data for themselves if they wish.

Writing reports: step three

Making recommendations

Most reports are commissioned because there is a problem which the commissioning editor would like addressed. Report writers collate and present information in order to find solutions. Each report should therefore include a list of recommendations, which, based on the report's findings, suggest possible courses of action for the future.

The executive summary

The main findings, interpretations and recommendations of the report should be summarised in this section. This summary is often placed towards the beginning of the report, after the Table of Contents, so that the reader can go straight to the key findings of the report without sifting through the detailed information presented.

Appendices

Any additional information, which would clutter up the report if it was placed in the main body of writing, but which readers might nevertheless find useful, should be placed in an Appendix at the end of the report. Appendices typically

173

include a discussion of the research methods employed, detailed statistical analyses, any questionnaires used, and/or more detailed results of the research. You should refer to the Appendices in the main body of the report whenever this is appropriate.

Acknowledgements

Remember also to acknowledge all those who have helped you in your research for the report.

SUMMARY OF HOW TO WRITE ESSAYS AND REPORTS

A good essay or report should be:

Structured – with introduction, review of the literature, argument and conclusion.
Theoretically informed – theories relevant to the essay must be outlined and discussed.
Focused – answering the question set.
Logically argued – points should be well linked and follow on from each other.
Clearly written – using your own style of writing, in your own words.
Well informed – use a wide range of reading/research.
Critical – exploring different and competing ways of looking at the question.
Convincing – statements should be backed up with evidence.
Referenced – all sources and ideas must be correctly acknowledged.

Chapter 21

Oral presentations

Occasionally you will be asked to present your work in an oral presentation. Many students do not like to present in this way, but it is a great skill to learn and very useful in other walks of life. The best way to build confidence in presenting is to get the preparation right so that you know exactly what you want to say. Oral presentations should be planned as carefully as if you were planning an essay or a report. Many of the skills which you have used for written work are useful in planning oral presentations too.

A good presentation should be:

Well informed – use a wide range of reading. You should research your presentations as well as you research for any other piece of work.

Structured – with introduction, argument and conclusion.

Theoretically informed – theories relevant to the presentation should be highlighted.

Focused – answering the presentation brief.

Logically argued – points should be well linked and follow on from each other.

Clearly presented – using your own words.

Critical – exploring different and competing ways of looking at the question.

Convincing – statements should be backed up with evidence.

How to present

The spoken word is very different from the written word. You will have to write your presentation as it is spoken, not as it would be written. Spoken presentations have to be very clear and concise and too much technical jargon avoided. Your points should be made clearly so that the audience understands them with ease. In an oral presentation the audience cannot stop you and ask you to repeat a point if they do not understand it the first time. This means that if you are presenting from a written piece of work you will have to rewrite it for the spoken word, you will not be able to just read it as it stands.

It is a good idea to emphasise important points in a presentation by *recapping*. This ensures that your audience understands which are the main points you are making. People who teach presentational skills often say that the presenter should:

- say what they are going to say
- say it
- summarise what they have said

While this may labour the point somewhat it is worth bearing in mind that you have to work hard to ensure that your audience is left at the end of the presentation with a clear idea of the points you have set out to make. It is easy for your audience's attention to wander, so it is worth re-emphasising salient points.

- Try to speak calmly and clearly when presenting. There should be plenty of pauses and breaks to help the audience absorb what you are saying and to emphasise certain points.
- Try not to read from a prepared script but to have remembered just what it is that you wish to say. Presenters who read the whole of their presentations often deliver their work in a very deadpan way. This does not help the audience to understand the points being made. Some presenters use cue cards so that they have the main points to be made on cards in front of them and they build their presentation around these.
- For the less accomplished speaker it can be a good idea to write the whole of the presentation using the exact words which you intend to use and to try to learn as much of it as possible. Then, if you 'dry up' in the middle because of nerves, or forget what you want to say, you will have something to read from. Just knowing that they have this backup if things go wrong can help build the presenter's confidence.
- Think how people change their emphasis, inflection and tone when they are in general conversation. These changes in tempo and tone are important when transmitting ideas orally and presenters are much more interesting if they can deliver their points in just such a conversational style.
- Illustrate your presentation with overhead slides, including tables, diagrams and images wherever possible. It helps if the audience can see visual images which help illustrate your point.

- If your overhead slides include text make sure this is in a large enough font for all of the audience to see, and do not put too much text on each slide.

TOP TIP

When presenting always have a copy of your overhead slides in front of you. Many presenters make the mistake of not preparing copies of the slides, so they look back at the projected image when talking. This means that they end up with their back to the audience. This can mean losing the attention of the audience or, if they are not using a microphone, that they are not projecting their voice towards the audience and it is difficult to hear what they are saying as a result.

Keeping to time

It is very important to keep to the time allotted for your presentation. It is always frustrating for the audience if a speaker overruns their time or if they rush their points at the end. It is always a good idea to practise the presentation, if possible in front of a willing audience, and to time how long each section takes to make sure that the presentation is neither too long nor too short and that you allow ample time to explain the main points.

TOP TIP

Plenty of practice makes for perfect presentations.

Using visual aids

Oral presentations are a great opportunity to indulge your creative side and to use visual aids to enhance your presentation. However, we have all seen overheads used poorly, with type that is so small it is difficult to read, or which detracts from the presentation rather than adding to it. There are certain rules which you should follow when designing and using visual aids, which will ensure that you use them effectively. These guidelines apply whether you are using

177

overhead transparencies or data projectors with your computer's presentation software.

- Keep your overheads simple.
- Make sure they can be seen by everyone in the room.
- Use large fonts, around 24 pt or above and bold type.
- Limit your text to as few words as possible.
- Use six or seven lines of text per overhead at the most.
- Use the overhead to emphasise what you are saying.
- Use graphs and charts to present data only when this enhances your point.

Do not use too many visual aids. As a rough estimate, you should use one for every five minutes of presentation. This gives the audience time to listen to what you are saying and read the information on the overhead. Any more than this will be too fast for your audience to assimilate.

Chapter 22

Communicating using tables and diagrams

You will often have to present complex data in your work. Although you can describe any data in the form of words, this can often be a long-winded and confusing method of getting your information across to your audience. Placing your data into tables, or into diagrammatic form can help to simplify and clarify the points which you are making. You should consider inserting tables and diagrams into your text wherever you think this might help the reader. The secret is to make your presentation of the data as clear and as simple as possible.

There are many different ways of presenting information in tables and diagrams. Here we look at some of the simplest and non-technical which you might use in reports, essays and other presentations.

Using tables

Tables can include numerical and written information and can be equally useful to help to demonstrate a theoretical point, and not only to aid the understanding of quantitative data.

Understanding qualitative information through the use of tables

Look at Table 22.1. It is adapted from R. K. Merton's (1957) book *Social Theory and Social Structure*.

This table helps us to understand some very complex theorising. Merton has suggested that young people tend to exhibit a variety of types of behaviour (a typology), some of which may lead them into offending. As well as describing the various types of behaviour which young people might display, he shows these in the form of a table, which helps to demonstrate a complex relationship in a very simple way.

To understand the table you need a 'key', i.e. an explanation of what the symbols + and − refer to. For this table + means that this group accepts, and − that the group rejects these modes of behaviour. The symbol ± means that this

Table 22.1 *Merton's typology of individual adaptation*

Modes of adaptation	Cultural goals	Legitimate means
Conformity	+	+
Innovation	+	−
Ritualism	−	+
Retreatism	−	−
Rebellion	±	±

Source: Adapted from Merton, R. K. (1957) *Social Theory and Social Structure.* New York: Free Press, p. 140

group not only rejects the behaviour but replaces it with behaviour based on a different set of values altogether. So we can see at a glance here that those in the conforming group accept society's cultural goals as well as attaining them through legitimate means, whilst those in the retreatist group, reject both.

Note that in this table there is a source for the information presented. ALL tables should include this. In this instance we have not used an exact replica of Merton's table, using his exact words and form of table, so we have signalled that it is an 'adaptation' of Merton's work.

Understanding quantitative information through the use of tables

Tables are also very often used to display quantitative information in a simple but effective manner. Suppose, for example, that we tested Merton's theory on a sample of 1,000 young people in Manchester. Imagine that we asked them a

Table 22.2 *Merton's typology of individual adaptation as found in a sample of 1,000 young people from Manchester in 2005*

Modes of adaptation	Numbers in group
Conformity	567
Innovation	123
Ritualism	110
Retreatism	57
Rebellion	243

Source: Evans, K. and King, D. (2005)

180

series of questions and used their answers to categorise them into Merton's groups. The (made-up) results could be displayed as shown in Table 22.2.

As you can see, displaying results in tables can very effectively transmit information to the reader in a simple and straightforward way.

Using diagrams

Both qualitative and quantitative information can be effectively expressed in diagrammatic form too.

Understanding qualitative information through the use of diagrams

Look at Figure 22.1 which is very well known amongst sociologists. It is based on data collected on the growth of the city of Chicago from the 1900s.

This is a simple, yet very effective way of illustrating how the 'concentric zones' which emanate from the urban centre – 'The Loop' – become increasingly residential, suburban and professional as we travel from the centre of cities to their outlying areas. Indeed it is a model for urban development which can be applied to a great many cities and towns.

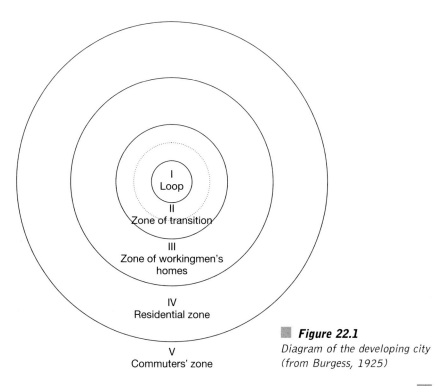

Figure 22.1
Diagram of the developing city (from Burgess, 1925)

Burgess has used a very simple design to illustrate, in diagrammatic form, what is actually quite a complex theoretical understanding. No wonder this has been so often copied by sociologists, geographers, urban planners and historians.

Understanding quantitative information through the use of diagrams

There are various simple diagrams which you can use to better display quantitative data. A few of the most basic designs are explained below:

Bar charts

Bar charts are some of the most simple, yet effective ways of presenting data. Bar charts can be presented on the vertical or the horizontal axis. Bar charts work best for items which you wish to directly compare. The bars must be in proportion to each other so that the relative proportions can be easily compared visually.

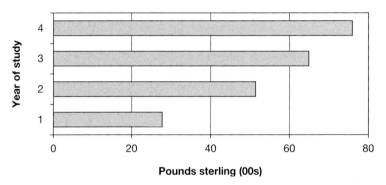

Figure 22.2 *Bar chart of a typical student's debt in the UK (1996–2000)*

Source: Evans and King (2004) *Demonstration Statistics*

From Figure 22.2 you can tell instantly how the level of a typical student's debt increases year on year. The chart shows that the typical student beginning their course of study in 1996 left their first year with over £2,000 of debt and that this rose to nearly £8,000 by the end of their fourth year. Although you could have described the data presented here in words, presenting it visually has the added advantage of demonstrating how the debt of a typical student mounts up year after year to reach its peak at nearly £8,000. The horizontal plane of the chart is particularly good at showing this.

The chart is clearly labelled so that the viewer can see exactly what information is included and that:

- It refers to the years 1996 to 2000 (this is in the title).
- It shows the debt at each year of study (vertical axis).
- It shows that the unit of measurement is pounds sterling (horizontal axis).
- It further shows that the debt is measured in the hundreds. The two noughts in the brackets mean that these should be added to the 20, 30, 40, 60 and 80 to make them 2,000, 3,000, 4,000, 6,000 and 8,000 respectively. This is called the 'unit of measurement'. It is much neater than using the larger numbers on the chart itself.
- The *source* of the data is also clearly shown (although in this case the data was made up for demonstration purposes).

Line graphs

We could also show how a typical student's debt rises over four years by using a line graph. Using the demonstration statistics presented above in Figure 22.2 a visual representation of the typical student's debt would look like the graph depicted in Figure 22.3.

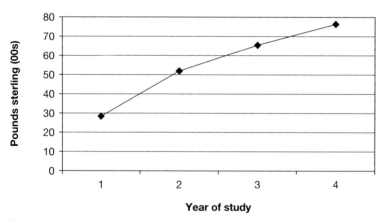

Figure 22.3 *Line graph of a typical student's debt in the UK (1996–2000)*
Source: Evans and King (2004) *Demonstration Statistics*

Here the axes are reversed so that the graph shows the level of debt rising as each year finishes. This furnishes the reader with another immediate pictorial representation of the rising debt and without losing any of the information presented.

Note that in this graph the points at which each year finishes are highlighted on the graph (as diamonds). This is because the data gives the level of debt at the end of each year. If we had looked at the rise in debt on a daily basis then we could have dispensed with these marked points and shown the graph as one continuous unmarked line.

183

Pie charts

These are the classic circles divided into segments. They are effective at showing the relative value of different variables in your data. So if you wished to show *how much* of a student's debt went to buy different items and to compare how much of a student's income is spent on leisure to the amount which is spent on rent, a pie chart would be ideal. It might look something like Figure 22.4.

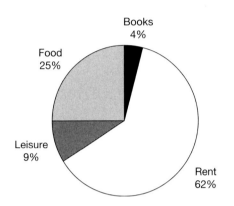

Books
4%

Food
25%

Leisure
9%

Rent
62%

Figure 22.4

Pie chart of how a typical student's debt was spent in the UK (1996–2000)

Source: Evans and King (2004)
Demonstration Statistics

This chart shows, in quite a dramatic fashion, that the majority of the typical student's income is being spent on rent and food. This data could therefore be used to counter any suggestion that rising student debt is a result of profligate spending on entertainment and nights out. The graphic representation of these figures is particularly good at making the point that students are accruing their debt mainly through purchasing the basic necessities, accommodation and food and are spending a relatively small amount on 'extras' such as leisure. Again, the graphical representation has been chosen to make the most of the data, to clarify the point made and to demonstrate something which comes across well visually. This can give the point you are making added emphasis.

Histograms

Histograms look very similar to bar charts but in a histogram each column denotes *a range* of values, rather than one value alone. For example, in Figure 22.5 the first bar shows all those students who left university with *between* £6,000 and £7,000 of debt, the second those who left with *between* £7,000 and £8,000 of debt, and so on. The amount of debt owed by all the students is represented by the area covered by each column. For this reason there is no space left between the columns.

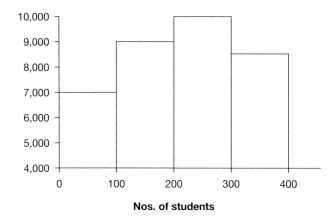

Figure 22.5
Histogram of the level of final student debt at Utopia University 2000 (£'000)

Source: Evans and King (2004) Demonstration Statistics

TOP TIP

Use visual representations of data to help to make a point more clearly (see Figures 22.1 to 22.5 above). Do not overuse them.

Note that in this chart the 'unit of measurement' is in the thousands of pounds (represented by the 3 noughts and the pound sterling sign in the brackets). This helps to simplify the chart even more but again it loses none of the information presented.

Using simple arithmetic

There are a number of very basic arithmetical techniques which you can use to help you to present your quantitative data in a more easily readable form. You can use these techniques to improve the look of tables, and when inserting statistical data into your essays and reports. In this section we are going to look at using:

1 rounding
2 percentages
3 averages

Rounding

You will often come across data written in quite a raw form. For example, figures showing Internet access worldwide are expressed in millions. Using such large

185

numbers is unwieldy, so the first thing you can do is to get rid of all those noughts at the end. Thus 1,255,000, that is one million two hundred and fifty-five thousand, can be expressed as 1.255 million, which is much easier to say, to write and to understand visually.

How to round

To decide where we put the decimal point we count how many noughts we use to express one million (1,000,000) – which is six. Then count six back from the end of the figure and place the decimal point there. We can then get rid of all the, now surplus, noughts which make the figure complicated to read. So to express a figure in the hundreds (100 has two noughts) count back two decimal points, in the thousands (1000 has three noughts) count back three decimal points and so on.

However, what if the number you are working with was more accurately represented as 1 255 063 and you wished to express this in millions to make it easier to use? Again count back six figures to place the decimal point after the 1 of one million and you come up with the figure of 1.255063 million. This is better, but not much because there are so many figures after the decimal point. In this instance you should 'round' the figure up or down to make it easier to express. This is done as follows:

1 Decide how many figures you want to use after the decimal point – in this example we will decide on three figures.
2 Take the figure to four decimal points, one more than you wish to use – this gives the figure of 1.2550.
3 Take away the last nought and the figure becomes 1.255 million.

However, what if the last figure is not a nought? Say for example that you decided to take the number to only two figures after the decimal point. In this case you should:

1 Take the figure to three decimal points, one more than you wish to use – this gives the figure of 1.255 and the last number is now a 5 which cannot just be discarded as a nought can.
2 If the last number is five or above, take it away and 'round up' the previous number to one more than it was previously, i.e. to give the figure of 1.26 million.
3 If the last number had been below five, i.e. 1.254, then you would 'round down' and merely take the number away as you did with the nought in the previous example and therefore 1,254,063 stays at 1.25 million.

Of course, you must let your reader know that you have 'rounded' the figures to whichever number of decimal points you have chosen.

TOP TIP

Use 'rounding' when the numbers with which you are working are long and complicated and you wish to express them more clearly. Do *not* use 'rounding' if it is important that you portray a figure as accurately as possible.

Percentages

It can often be useful to express figures as percentages. Percentages are figures expressed as a proportion of the total amount and the convention is to use 100 as the base for the total figure – per cent means 'out of 100'. Percentages are calculated as follows:

Example 1

In the easiest example, the total figure *would* actually be 100. So, imagine that you ask 100 people how fearful they are of walking alone at night in their neighbourhood. Sixty-three people tell you that they are not afraid at all. This means that 63 out of 100, or 63% were not afraid at all.

Example 2

But what if you asked 1,000 people the same question and 630 said they were not afraid at all. This is still 63% of the total who say that they are not at all afraid, but do you know how you worked this out? There is an easy formula which you can use to express figures in percentages.

1 Take the number you want to express as a percentage (x).
2 Divide this by the total number (y).
3 Multiply your answer by 100.

In this case

x = 630 (this is the number of people who are not afraid)

and

y = 1,000 (this is the total number of people asked)

so the calculation is:

1 630
2 divided by 1,000
3 multiplied by 100

187

And you have shown that out of 1,000 people asked, 63% were not afraid of walking alone at night in their neighbourhood.

Example 3

Now we have the basic formula we can express more complicated figures as percentages and use this to compare the responses of different groups.

Imagine that of the 1,000 people whom you interviewed 488 were female and 512 were male. Of these 301 females and 329 males said that they were not at all afraid of walking in their neighbourhood at night.

Which group, males or females, are more likely to say that they are not afraid of walking alone at night?

This is difficult to tell by looking at these raw figures alone – the numbers, after all are quite close, so we express the figures as percentages in order to better compare the answers given.

Using the formula above this is quite simple. We work out the percentage of women who are not afraid, and then we work out the percentage of men who are not afraid and compare the two.

For females:

$x = 301$ (this is the number of females who say that they are not afraid)

and

$y = 488$ (this is the total number of females asked)

So:

1 Apply the formula, so that x is divided by y and multiplied by 100, so: 301 divided by 488 multiplied by 100 gives us 61.68.
2 'Round' this figure to make it easier to understand, we will use no decimal points here, this gives us 62.
3 The percentage of women who say that they are not at all afraid is **62%**.

For males: $x = 329$ and $y = 512$

So:

4 Apply the formula and 329 divided by 512 multiplied by 100 gives us 64.25.
5 'Round' this figure to make it easier to understand, again we will dispense with the decimal points, this gives us 64.
6 The percentage of men who say that are not at all afraid is **64%**.

188

This is much easier to understand. We can now directly compare the figures and see that slightly more males (64%) say that they are not at all afraid of walking in their neighbourhood at night than women (62%).

TOP TIP

Use percentages when you want to make it easy to make comparisons across your data but the groups you are comparing are not equal in size.

Averages

Averages are a little more complicated because there is more than one type. Basically the term average refers to the value around which a set of values are centred. But this is quite hard to understand, so here we will look in more detail at the following to clarify what the term 'average' can mean:

1 the mean
2 the mode
3 the median

Example 1 The mean

This is the most commonly used definition of average. It is easily calculated, by adding up all the values in a distribution and then dividing by the number of values present.

Say, for example, you have the annual salaries of 15 social workers and you wished to find out the 'average' pay awarded to this set of social workers. To calculate the 'mean' pay, you would add all the salaries together and divide the total by 15 to find the 'average' pay for that group.

19 768	21 023	21 023	23 086	23 086
23 086	23 086	24 089	26 785	26 785
32 976	32 976	38 765	38 765	41 111

The total number of all these salaries added together is: 416 410.00
Divide this by 15 and the 'average' pay is: 27 760.67

You can then use this figure to make other interesting calculations, for example to discover how many are paid above and how many below the 'average' rate.

189

Example 2 The median

The median refers to the mid-point of a distribution of values. It can be useful when your list of values includes some outliers. For example, our list of 15 salaries may be grouped around 27 000 but a few are above 30 000 and one is at 19 000. It does not make sense to look at the simple arithmetic mean of these salaries because the group is skewed by these extreme values. However, the median point is exactly the half-way point in the distribution, so it gives a more useful average. It can be easily calculated thus:

Step One: Arrange the salaries in ascending order, like so:

19 768
21 023
21 023
23 086
23 086
23 086
23 086
24 089
26 785
26 785
32 976
32 976
38 765
38 765
41 111

Step Two: Divide the number of salaries plus one by two, i.e. 15 + 1 divided by 2 = 8.

Step Three: Take the eighth salary in this order as the median, i.e. 24 089.

Imagine there were an even number of salaries. In this case we disregard the last salary in the list for this purpose.

The median would then be 13 + 1 divided by 2 = 7.
In this case the median would be the seventh salary in the list.

So this is quite a different number to the 'mean' salary and means that most social workers earn something near this salary. The average salary, calculated through the arithmetical mean, appeared higher because three social workers earned quite a lot more than the other 12.

190

TOP TIP

The median is easy to calculate if you only have a few cases to analyse but is best left to computer software to calculate if you have a large number of cases. However, you should now understand what the median is, why it is useful and when you should consider using it rather than using a simple arithmetical mean.

Example 3 The mode

This measure of average can be even more complicated to calculate and could easily be left to computer software, but it is important that you understand when it should be used above the mean or the median. The mode refers to the most often found value in a list. If, for example, you were ordering shoes for a shop and wanted to know which size of shoe would be most likely to sell the most, then there would be little use in knowing either the mean of the shoe sizes sold or the median, instead you would want to know the most popular shoe size. With a small data set you can find the mode by listing how many times a value appears, that which appears most often is the mode. For example in a shoe warehouse the following numbers of shoes (categorised by size) are sold in a single year.

Size 6	566,039
Size 7	867,002
Size 8	998,056
Size 9	752, 039

In this example it is easy to see that the most popular size sold is a Size 8.

Descriptive statistics

The charts, graphs and arithmetical calculations which have been shown here are all referred to as *descriptive statistics*. That is they help us to *describe* the data which we have available to us. They do not allow us to *generalise* or to *infer* that what we have described would be true for all similar groups. They are very basic statistical techniques and there are many others which are more advanced but not covered in this introductory book. It is important, however, that you practise using these basic techniques and get to know when each is relevant to a particular set of data.

191

There are some exercises on the website for you to try out. These will help you to familiarise yourself with these basic statistical techniques and to become more comfortable with them.

TOP TIP

Whether you are using tables and diagrams to help you present quantitative or qualitative data *REMEMBER*:

- Always give your table or diagram a heading which accurately describes its contents.
- Always give the source for your data.
- Give row and column headings in tables.
- Keep them simple.

In addition, when using tables or diagrams to show quantitative data:

- Round numbers to make them easier to understand.
- Try to use no more than two decimal points.
- Give your unit of measurement.
- Give percentages where you wish to make comparisons between groups.
- Label your vertical and horizontal axes in diagrams.

Chapter 23

Communicating via the Internet

Over the past few years computers have become tools which help us to communicate with each other. Many people have found email to be an extremely efficient form of communication. Emails can be used to keep in touch with friends or as important ways to communicate information within or between institutions. You may be very familiar with email software but there are various ways to make your email communication even more effective.

Emailing an individual

Emailing to an individual person is quite straightforward once you have understood the software. However we find students often make a number of errors or omissions that render their email messages less effective than they could be.

Subject headings

These should always be filled in and should reflect the subject matter of the email and its relative urgency. It is easy to forget when sending an email that the receiver of the message may get hundreds of emails in one day. They will not always be able to read everything that is sent to them, so the sender should consider how to ensure that their message is one of those read. The receiver may well 'scan' the subject headings to find those of interest, so make sure that yours is filled in and does attract their attention. If the message is urgent then this can also be signalled in the heading.

Signature files

Always sign off your email in an appropriate way. Make sure the receiver of the email knows exactly who you are. Sometimes people forget that they have not used their own name in their email address and then do not 'sign' their emails. So there is a chance that the receiver will not know who you are. You should always make sure that you give your name at the end of an email. Sometimes, however, your name alone will not identify you sufficiently and you need to give some more information such as your status and the institution for which you work. I have been told by some people that I have contacted through email that this information was very important to them in deciding whether to reply.

Most email software allows you to write a 'signature file' which will be automatically appended to every message that you send. This can be extremely useful so that you do not have to remember to identify yourself every time you send a message. These signature files can also be used to personalise messages. Some people include quotes, perhaps from a favourite book or some lyrics to a record, to their signature files. Such quotes can help to say something to the receiver of your messages about the sort of person that you are, much as other things like choice of clothing, badges worn, etc. can signify something about the sort of person you are to those whom you meet in person.

Attaching files

Emails are very useful for sending all sorts of computer files to other people, whether these are word-processed documents, images or any other data file. As long as the recipient has the same software they will be able to open up your documents without a problem. Most email packages have a paperclip icon on their tool bar. After writing the email, click this button and this allows you to attach a file to your email. The file will be sent at the same time as the email. This is a particularly good way to share files, especially if you are sharing writing with another person, who can then read the file, edit it where appropriate and then send it back to you.

Sending files to other people can be a good way to backup any important files which you do not wish to lose. Check with the recipient first, though, as some attached files can take some time to download at the other end, especially if the recipient has a slow connection to the Internet.

Send files in their most basic format. *You* may have the latest computer software installed on your machine but this is not necessarily true for your recipient.

Sending email to more than one person

Before the Internet most communication tools were interpersonal. Tools such as the letter, telegraph or telephone allowed contact between individuals who were separated by space. Individuals could contact each other through all these means but if they wanted to exchange their ideas with a group of people this was more laborious and communiqués had to be copied to all those involved. The only way to have a group discussion was to field a conference telephone call or to meet in person. All other mass communication was a one-way broadcast only, i.e. using the television or radio, and these did not allow two-way conversations. Email has changed all this and allowed groups of people to communicate in various ways. Some of these are explained below.

Address books

Use the address book included with your email software. It is a good idea to find out how the address book in your email software works. You should be able to record all the email addresses of the people with whom you correspond here. This means that you will not have to remember and write their email address every time you write to them. You can open up your address book instead and click on the name of the person you want to write to. This feature becomes especially important when you want to send the same email to a group of people – instead of writing all their addresses you can just click on each name in turn.

However, you should also learn how to set up group email lists. You can do this by grouping together a number of email addresses under a main heading, sometimes referred to as a nickname which identifies the group. Then, when you insert the nickname into the Send To box, your email will automatically be sent to everyone in that group. This can save a great deal of time as well as cutting down on errors which can occur when sending emails to large groups of people.

Cc and Bcc

Did you know that the Cc line which most email software includes refers to Carbon Copy. If you add an email address to this line, an identical copy of your email will be sent to that address. You can put more than one email address or nickname in this box to send any number of identical emails out. The email that the recipient receives will include all this information so that they know who else has received a copy.

Bcc refers to Blind Carbon Copy, so if you add an email address or nickname to this line, you can send an identical copy of the email to some other person or group of people but this time the recipients will not know that you have sent a copy to anyone else.

Listservs

These are email lists which are set up more centrally in an institution and which are therefore open to more than one person to use. Those which you set up using your own address books will only be available to you and you will have to update them as relevant; but listservs are maintained and updated centrally and can be used by anyone given authority to so do.

195

Mailing lists

These can be found on the Internet. These are places where people from all over the world can share ideas and interests.

Mailing lists can be extremely useful, especially if all the list members take their subject seriously; but they can also be frustrating and can be misused and stray wildly from the given topic. People 'post' their questions or thoughts on a subject by sending an email to the list which is then sent out to everyone who has 'subscribed' to the list through their email. This can often lead to a detailed discussion on a selected topic. The postings are often 'archived', i.e. put somewhere on the web so that anyone can read what past discussions have been about. Most serious mailing lists have moderators or editors who filter out any irrelevant or offensive postings.

Unless someone has told you about a useful list, you will have to search one of the list databases that are available on the web to find a mailing list which is relevant to you. Some of these databases have information on over 50,000 mailing lists but it may be possible to search for lists on particular topics. Some lists can be quite busy with many 'postings' sent each day; others can be very quiet indeed. If you join a busy list you can usually reduce the amount of email you receive by opting to receive a digest rather than individual emails. That means that you will get one email periodically which contains all postings for that period.

To get some idea of the number of lists and the topics covered have a look at *Tile.Net* (http://www.tile.net/lists/). As you will see, many lists are not likely to be of much help in your studies. *Google groups* (http://groupsbeta.google.com/) and *Yahoo groups* (http://groups.yahoo.com/) are also popular places to locate email lists, although, again, most of them will be concerned with leisure activities rather than with topics that might help your studies.

There are, however, some databases of email lists which are geared towards more academic concerns. *JISCmail* (http://www.jiscmail.ac.uk/) is a mailing list service for the UK Higher and Further Education communities. H-Net (http://www.h-net.org/lists/) was originally more concerned with history but now it covers the humanities and social sciences more generally. It tends to focus on the USA. *CataList* is the catalogue of the 54,416 public LISTSERV email lists which can be found on the World Wide Web (http://www.lsoft.com/catalist.html).

Each list database looks different, but all will allow you to search from a general subject database, or to put in your own search terms. You should link your terms with Boolean operators in order to get the best results. So if you are looking for an email list on White water rafting, use:

white AND water AND rafting

as your search term. Or try putting the phrase in quotation marks. The engine will then search for the exact phrase:

'white water rafting'.

When you have located a list, the database will give you the information you need to 'subscribe', i.e. to get on the mailing list. This usually involves sending an email to the list with an exactly reproduced message in it. The message is often 'subscribe list', but you will be told what form of words to use. If you put anything else in the message it will not work, so make sure you remove an automated signature on your email if you have one. If you successfully subscribe, you will receive an email to say that you are on the list and, most importantly, to tell you how to leave it. Keep this message – you never know when you might want it!

You should then start to receive messages from the mailing list which you have chosen. If you decide to send your own message into the list, make full use of the Subject line when sending your email. This is like giving your message a title, so that everyone else on the list has an idea of what is in the message before they open it. If you are replying to a message, then keep the same subject heading so that everyone knows that the two messages are linked in some way.

You can also use the databases given above to read and follow 'archived' discussions, i.e. discussions that happened before you joined a mailing list, but which are still held in a database. In fact it is a good idea to take a look at the archives before joining a list so that you can decide if it is really what you are looking for. It is also a good idea to look at the archives before asking a question in case it has already been discussed.

Newsgroups and Bulletin Boards

Newsgroups and Bulletin Boards are quite similar to mailing lists. They are also similar to on-line discussion groups but their messages are not automatically sent out to all members, instead all the messages are kept on a 'server' which it is necessary for you to 'visit' to see what has been posted.

The term 'Newsgroup' is actually misleading. Newsgroups can be used to disseminate news but most function as discussion forums on different topics. They work in a different way to mailing lists. With Newsgroups all the messages are held on a 'server' – they are not transmitted to you via email, so you have to find them and connect to them in order to read the messages. Your Internet service provider may provide the software to user newsgroups but this varies depending on the newsgroup you are using, so you must check to see what arrangements are applicable to you.

When you have accessed your newsreader software you need to find what groups are likely to be of interest to you. Here are two websites where you can start looking:

- TILE.NET/NEWS (http://www.tile.net/news/)
- Harley Hahn's Master List of Usenet Newsgroups (http://www.harley.com/usenet/)

197

You can, however, access newsgroups though your web browser in the same way as you access other Internet pages. Google Groups eliminates the need for newsreading software. Go to http://groups-beta.google.com/ and type in your search terms. If you find a group that interests you, you can look at the postings, but if you wish to post to the group you will have to set up a (free) Google account.

Newsgroups are arranged in hierarchies and you are given a clue as to which are interesting by the titles of the discussion groups. First, the newsgroups are sorted into wide categories, e.g. education, science, business, etc. Each of these wider categories has a particular prefix or suffix, for example:

edu = education
biz = business
soc = connected to social issues
rec = recreational

Secondly, the newsgroup will be given a name which explains in more detail what is being covered in the discussion, e.g. **alt.music.badlydrawnboy** – which is a bit of a giveaway; obviously people in this discussion list are interested in discussing the music of Badly Drawn Boy. Some are less obvious: alt.crime.bail-enforce proved to be someone from the United States who wanted to make money as an enforcer of bail conditions and was asking for advice. Needless to say, the first of these had more 'postings'.

When someone posts to a newsgroup they give their message a heading, e.g. 'Radiohead's latest CD'. Then everyone who visits the site will know that the message relates to the latest musical offerings of that group. You can reply directly to that posting, or start another topic of discussion which is signalled by a different subject heading. Once a discussion has started on a particular topic this becomes known as a 'thread'. This means that you do not have to read *all* the messages posted to the newsgroup, but can focus on one or another particular 'thread'.

We have included Newsgroups here because you need to know about them and you can sometimes find useful information there. But because anyone can

TOP TIP

If you wish to try out some mailing lists and newsgroups then go to the website where you will find a number of places which host mailing lists on the web. Each allows you to search for a mailing list of interest by inserting keywords into a text box. You can then 'subscribe' to a list of your choice and start receiving emails. If you decide to send your own message then make full use of the subject heading boxes. This will allow your message to be archived in the relevant 'thread'

198

post to them and there is no censorship or control, many of them are full of spam, offensive material or just plain rubbish.

'Netiquette': rules of the game

The Internet is a relatively new communications tool and we are still learning how to use it. It is not quite speech, not quite the written word, but somewhere between the two. As it is so new we have not really developed any rules governing its use – so it is quite an anarchic space and many people like it just for that reason. However, when you are using the Internet to communicate with people you do not know very well, it is worth sticking to some simple rules to avoid upsetting other Internet users and to make sure that you get your points across as effectively as possible. These rules have been termed 'netiquette'.

'Netiquette' refers to network etiquette or how to behave properly on-line. It is basically about remembering that there are real people out there and you should behave responsibly and afford them the same respect that we hope you give to others who you don't meet on-line. There are also a few rules which relate to the peculiarities of Internet communication. You will gradually get used to them. If you make a mistake and upset someone don't worry – just say sorry!

TOP TIPS: SOME WEB GUIDES TO NETIQUETTE

Netiquette Home Page (http://www.albion.com/netiquette/)
Netmanners.com (http://www.netmanners.com)
Learnthenet (http://www.learnthenet.com/english/html/09netiqt.htm)
European Telework Online (http://www.eto.org.uk/rules.htm)

Some basic Netiquette rules:

- Keep your message short.
- Only reply if you have something new to add.
- Make sure your message is relevant to the general topic area of the list.
- Use the 'subject' line so that people can decide if they want to read your email or not and it will also help them to follow the 'thread' of a topic.
- Write clearly – remember that people whose first language is not English may be reading your message.
- Do not write in uppercase. It is interpreted as shouting or expressing anger.
- Use plain text. Using fancy colours, fonts and so on can make it difficult or impossible for some readers to read your message.
- It is sometimes helpful to quote from a previous message if you are replying to it. But try to do this sparingly. It is not usually necessary to quote the whole of a message.

199

Chapter 24

Acknowledging the work of others

Earlier we looked at how all work is produced in an academic and social context. This means that we do not start any piece of work from scratch. Our ideas are informed by what we have read, what we have experienced and conversations we have had with other people. Some of these sources will have to be referenced but this is not always an easy or straightforward task. First of all it is important to know which sources should be referenced, and then to ensure that you reference systematically and accurately. It will not be possible, or indeed necessary, to reference all sources for your ideas. Look at the following exercise to help you to decide which sources should be accurately referenced: there then follows some suggested answers.

EXERCISE 24.1 WHEN TO REFERENCE

Look at the following scenarios and decide if you should reference the source of these ideas and how each source might be referenced:

Scenario 1
You are participating in a seminar at university and in the course of the discussion a student presents some information which makes you think differently about a particular subject. You later incorporate these new ideas into a piece of writing. Your ideas have been influenced and informed by a third party – do you need to reference the seminar?

Scenario 2
You are attending a public lecture, the speaker presents some ideas which you later incorporate into an essay. Should this lecture be included in your references?

Scenario 3

You are writing an essay and decide to conduct some research on the Internet. In the course of this research you join a chatroom on a subject relevant to your essay. The postings of one of the participants helps you think differently about the subject you are studying. Do you reference this chatroom posting?

Scenario 4

You come across an interesting theory in a journal article. You have just written something very similar in your essay as your own research has led you to think along these lines already and you feel that this article confirms everything that you already believed about this subject. Is this idea your own, or should you reference the article, which after all only confirms what you were already thinking?

EXERCISE 24.1   SUGGESTED ANSWERS

Scenario 1 Answer – No

As a rule private conversations do not have to be referenced. A discussion which takes place in a university seminar group does not take place in the public domain and would therefore be considered a private conversation. However, you need to carefully consider what the student said which influenced you. Did he or she present some data which influenced your ideas? If so, what was the source of that data? Should you look at this data yourself to check the accuracy of that student's interpretation? Did she refer to a piece of work which she had read? You should consider reading this work for yourself as it appears to shed useful insights into the subject with which you are concerned. You should then reference the data or work which you subsequently use to inform your own writing.

Scenario 2 Answer – Yes

This discussion has taken place in the public domain and should be referenced accordingly with speaker, title, date and place of presentation accurately recorded.

Scenario 3 Answer – Possibly

This scenario is the most ambiguous and you must use your judgement here. An Internet chatroom might be considered to take place in the public domain, especially if the group is open to anyone to join. However, the 'conversations' that take place in a chatroom are often quite informal and 'off the cuff'. You must decide for yourself how formal the chatroom posting was intended to be. If it is a chatty riposte to another posting it may be excessive to reference it; however, if it is a well worked through and more formal response to a serious Internet-based discussion then you should consider referencing. Any direct quotations from chatrooms should always be fully referenced with author, date of posting, full details identifying the chatroom and where it can be found on the Internet, and the date on which you accessed the chatroom, all accurately recorded.

Scenario 4 Answer – Yes
You have come across this idea in the public domain in a published work. Regardless as to whether you too were coming to the same conclusion you must now reference the work

From the above exercises a number of principles have begun to emerge which you should use in order to make the decision as to whether to reference an idea, conversation or other person's data.

You should *always reference* your source as accurately as possible if:

- you have come across the idea or data in the public domain, *unless* it is considered to be *common knowledge* (see definition below);
- it has been published in a book, journal, newspaper, Internet site or any other publicly available documentation;
- you have quoted directly from a source;
- it is an idea which you have 'borrowed' from someone else, whether you use their words directly or have paraphrased their ideas.

WHAT IS 'COMMON KNOWLEDGE'?

Certain 'facts' are commonly known, usually because they come from knowledge based on common experiences. For example, we all know that mountain climbing is a risky occupation – we hardly need to reference the source of this knowledge, we read about climbing accidents in the news and we can see for ourselves that climbing up vertical rock faces poses inherent dangers.

However, we should also be very careful about using 'common knowledge' without verifying its truthfulness or accuracy. How risky is climbing exactly?

Is climbing more dangerous than crossing the road? And how could you find out? Some examples of 'common knowledge' are actually based on inaccurate data or misinformation. It is good practice to try not to rely on common knowledge and to research the facts behind seemingly uncontentious statements.

Why reference?

One of the main reasons for referencing sources is to avoid accusations of plagiarism (see below). However, there are other, equally as important reasons to reference the ideas and work of other people.

- Research is a collective effort, when we research we build on the work of other people. We will often refer to that work as an exemplary or interesting piece of research which we want to guide other people towards.
- When we try to understand the world around us and build theories about the way it works we want to incorporate as much knowledge as we can. We can use the work of other people to inform our own ideas. This means that we do not have to reinvent the wheel every time we set out to write. The work of others can be used to great effect to inform our own views. When this is the case it is right to acknowledge the work that we are building on.
- When writing a short paper we do not have the time and word length to explain all past knowledge in the subject area in detail. We can refer to well-known theories and the work of others so that we can move more quickly on to our own research and analysis. When exploring media coverage of crime, for example, we can refer to the concept of 'deviancy amplification' (Wilkins 1964). This concept, which explains the way in which misinformation and excessive reporting of certain offences leads to a disproportionate amount of attention paid to these offences rather than others, has been much used by criminologists. Its meaning is now widely understood so that the term can now be used, if referenced to its original source, as a kind of shorthand.
- A well-referenced work demonstrates that the author has read widely around a topic and that they are not relying on their own views and experiences alone or relying on a narrow area of the field. You can demonstrate your own breadth of reading by referencing other people's work throughout your own writing.
- A well-researched piece of work will reference the key thinkers in an area. This demonstrates that you are aware of the work of these theorists

203

and that you have taken this into consideration when formulating your own ideas and arguments.

- Good use of references can show that you are able to collect information from a variety of sources, select relevant data and incorporate these into your own work. This is a useful and key skill to learn in the course of your studies.
- The reader of your work may well want to go back to the original sources which you use, in order to follow up an argument or to check the original material or to use aspects of the work themselves at a later date.

If you bear in mind these reasons for referencing while you are writing you will quickly pick up this skill. It is important to remember that we rarely write for ourselves alone. We write in order to communicate ideas to other people. When writing any piece of work it is essential to consider the reader of the piece. It is important to make your arguments clear, to show the reader where your ideas come from, which writers you are using to help you frame your ideas and which ideas are original.

How to reference

Whenever you reference a work, whether as part of a bibliography or within the text of your work this must be accurately and consistently carried out. Think of your referencing as leaving a paper trail so that any reader can find all the works that you reference with ease. There are certain conventions which must be followed and which will help any reader locate the source of the ideas which you are using. All references must be complete and accurate, with author, date of publication, place of publication and publisher recorded. Referencing can be quite complicated – how are internet sites referenced, for example, or newspapers or government reports? The Harvard system of referencing is often used by social scientists and this is explained below and used in subsequent examples.

Bibliographies

Referencing books

These are usually the easiest sources to reference but even these are not always straightforward. The convention for referencing books is:

AUTHOR'S SURNAME, INITIALS. (Year of publication) *Title of publication*. Place of publication: Publisher.

Note the exact convention in placing commas, full stops, colons and where to italicise and use capital letters. So a reference for a book should be written as below:

204

BAUMAN, Z. (2001) *Community. Seeking safety in an insecure world.* Cambridge: Polity Press.

Now the reader can see at a glance who has written the book, when, what the book is titled, where it was published and by which organisation. This format may seem obvious but each component plays its own part in helping the reader track down the publication. In addition, each component can become more complicated. We will look at each now in turn:

Multiple authorship   If there is more than one author, then be sure to reproduce the order of authors as this has been written by the publishers as below:

BARON, S., FIELD, J. and SCHULLER, T. (2000) *Social Capital. Critical Perspectives.* Oxford: Oxford University Press.

Edited volumes   Edited volumes are a collection of pieces written by a variety of authors. When using any work from an edited volume you should ensure that the details of the complete volume are recorded in your bibliography. Make sure that you include (ed) after the named editor or (eds) if there is more than one named editor, as below:

BELL, C. and ROBERTS, H. (eds) (1984) *Social Researching: politics, problems, practice.* London: Routledge.

Reprinted books   Some classic texts are reprinted again and again. Each time the typescript may be altered so that page numbers change, or some editions will have addendums or different introductory chapters. It is important to identify exactly which edition you have used for your work and to give this information after the title, as below:

DAVIS, M. (2000) *Ecology of Fear. Los Angeles and the Imagination of Disaster.* 2nd ed. London: Macmillan.

The information which you need to reference correctly will often be found on the Title Page of a book or report. If you are using other media such as videos, television or radio programmes, however, this information may be more difficult to locate.

Referencing contributions in books, journals and conferences

Chapters in edited books   You will need to give full details of the chapter you are using as well as those of the edited volume in which the chapter can be found. Use the convention:

AUTHOR'S SURNAME, INITIALS. (Year of publication) 'Title of chapter' in: EDITOR'S SURNAME, INITIALS. (ed or eds if more than one editor) Title of book, Place of publication: Publisher, page numbers of contribution.

This will allow the reader to go straight to the chapter and/or pages in the book in which the work can be found. A referenced chapter should conform to the example below:

ADAM, A. AND GREEN. E. (1998) 'Gender, agency, location and the new information society' in B. Loader (ed) *Cyberspace Divide, Equality, Agency and Policy in the Information Society*. London: Routledge, pp.141–179.

Articles in journals   You will need to give full details of the article as well as the journal in which the article can be found. Journals are often published four times each year and given different volume numbers, so you will have to make sure that you include all the necessary information. Use the convention:

AUTHOR'S SURNAME, INITIALS. (Year of publication) 'Title of article' *Title of journal*, Volume number (section if relevant), page numbers of article.

A referenced article should conform to the example below:

FISHER B., MARGOLIS M. AND RESNICK D. (1996) 'Breaking Ground on the Virtual Frontier: Surveying life on the Internet' *American Sociologist*, Vol. 27 Spring, pp.11–29.

Conference papers   You might also wish to cite a paper which was delivered at a conference. You should contact the author to obtain a copy of the paper which you are interested in. You should then reference it as below:

RANERUP, A. (2000) 'A Comparative Study of On-Line Forums in Local Government in Sweden'. Paper presented to *Community Informatics Conference: Connecting communities through the web*. Middlesbrough, 26–28 April 2000, CIRA: University of Teesside.

Conference proceedings   Some conference papers are published in collections referred to as conference proceedings. For referencing purposes the volume of conference proceedings should be treated as if it were a book and the paper as though it were a chapter in that book. The reference might look like that below:

AICHHOLZER, G. AND SCHMUTZER, R. (1999) 'Options, policy issues and implementation of electronic government services' in J. Armitage and J. Roberts (eds) in: *Exploring Cyber-Society*. Volume 1, 5–7 July 1999, University of Northumbria at Newcastle, pp.56–68.

Referencing other written sources

Organisational material You will no doubt sometimes use material which is published by an organisation such as a government department or a private company. This should be referenced just as accurately as any academic work but instead of recording an author's name, you must include the organisation's details. You should use the convention:

> NAME OF ORGANISATION (Year of publication) *Title of publication*. Place of publication: Publisher, Report Number (if applicable).

The reference should conform to the example below:

> COMMISSION FOR RACIAL EQUALITY (1984) *Race and Council Housing in Hackney. Report of a Formal Investigation*. London: Commission for Racial Equality.

Theses Students completing postgraduate work are often required to write and to publish final theses. These are then placed in the library of the university which awards them their degree. These can then be located and used by any other student. They should then be referenced using the convention set out below:

> AUTHOR'S SURNAME, INITIALS. (Year of publication) *Title of thesis*. Thesis (Designation, i.e. PhD, Masters). University to which thesis submitted.

The reference should conform to the example below:

> GRAHAM, S. (1996) *Networking the City: A Comparison of Urban Tele-communications Initiatives in France and Britain*. Thesis (PhD). University of Manchester.

Newspaper articles

> AUTHOR (Year of publication) Heading of article *Newspaper* Date of news-paper. Page number of article.

The reference should conform to the examples given below:

> McELVOGUE, L. (1997) Bright sites, big city *The Guardian On-Line Section*. 20th February 1997. p.21.

Or if the author of the article is not given:

> THE GUARDIAN (1997) Bright sites, big city. 20th February 1997. p.21.

207

Referencing audio-visual material

Of course types of material other than the written word can be used as useful sources for research and writing. Referencing conventions are more relaxed for audio-visual material. However, be sure to leave as much information as possible so that the reader should be able to find the source material themselves.

For film or video

> *Title of film* (Year in which first released) Type of material, e.g. Film or video. DIRECTOR. Place of production: Producing organisation.

The following reference refers to a video which was put together by a collective and therefore has no one director. Its place of production is not recorded by the collective, although an email address allows the reader to contact the collective directly to obtain a copy.

> *Argentina in Revolt* (2002) VHS Video. A MASS PRODUCED VIDEO. Massproduced@artserve.net.

For television or radio programmes

> *Title of programme* (Year of broadcast) Number and title of episode. Medium, e.g. TV or Radio. Date of broadcast.

The reference should conform as closely as possible to the example below:

> *Six Feet Under* (2002) Episode 7. Brotherhood. TV. 22nd July 2002.

Contributions within television or radio programmes   You might wish to cite a television interview or a contribution made in a programme. Again follow the usual conventions as below:

> CONTRIBUTOR (Year of broadcast) Type of contribution. In: *Title of programme.* Medium. Channel. Date of broadcast. Time of broadcast.

As below:

> JACKSON, S.L. (2002) Interview. In: *Panorama.* TV, BBC1. 22nd July 1997. 23.05hrs.

For CD-Roms or DVDs

> AUTHOR or EDITOR (Year of publication) *Title of CD-Rom or DVD* Medium, e.g. CD-Rom or DVD (Edition) Place of publication: Publisher.

The reference should conform to the example below:

THE SPECIALS (1996) *Too Much, Too Young* CD-Rom. UK: EMI Records.

Referencing Internet-based sources

The internet is such a new medium that conventions for referencing such sources have not yet been fully established. However, it is vitally important to reference websites and email discussions as accurately as possible, giving the complete URLs (web addresses) of each page which you use so that the reader can locate the same website as easily as possible. Material on the web is often updated, moved to another location, or disappears from the web altogether. For that reason there is an additional piece of information which you must always include – that is the **date upon which you accessed the material** which you are citing. Use the conventions set out below.

For websites

AUTHOR or ORGANISATION (Year of writing if known, otherwise year site accessed) Title of webpage. Full URL of webpage [Date website accessed].

The reference should conform to the example below:

CARVIN, A. (2000) Beyond Access: Understanding the Digital Divide http://www.benton.org/Divide/thirdact/speech.html [Accessed 21.08.00].

For articles in electronic journals

AUTHOR'S SURNAME, INITIALS (Year of publication) 'Title of article.' *Title of journal* Volume and section, if relevant. Available from: full URL of article [Date website accessed].

The reference should conform to the example below:

SCHUSTER, L. AND SOLOMOS, J. (2001) 'Asylum, Refuge and Public Policy: Current Trends and Future Dilemmas' *Sociological Research Online* Volume 6, Issue 1. Available from: http://www.socresonline.org.uk [Accessed 23.07.02].

For discussion on email lists

AUTHOR'S SURNAME, INITIALS (Date of posting) Subject of posting, as given in the subject line. *Name of discussion list*. Available From: URL [Date Accessed].

209

The reference should conform to the example below:

> EVANS, K. (11.11.01) Having trouble referencing? *Studying Society Discussion List* Available from: http://www.liv.ac.uk/sociology/studyingsociety/ bboard [23.07.02].

For personal email communications

> SENDER'S SURNAME, INITIALS (Sender's email address)(Date of email) *Subject of message*, Email to: recipient (Recipient's email address).

> KING, B.B. (b.b.king@liv.ac.uk)(23.07.02) *London, England*, Email to: D.Ross (Ross@liv.ac.uk).

Citing sources in your text

When to cite

As well as constructing a full bibliography referencing all the material which you have used in your work, you will have to ensure that you reference or 'cite' all ideas, quotations, statements, theories, etc. which you use within your text. The work of other people should be cited at all times, whether you directly quote from the author, or whether you paraphrase or summarise their ideas. Again the Harvard system is probably the easiest and most commonly used citation system in the social sciences, so it is this system which is demonstrated below.

How to cite one author

The work of other people is cited in your text by recording the author's (or editor's) surname followed by the date of the publication as in (King 1998).

How to cite multiple works by the author

The date of the publication which you are citing will normally be enough to distinguish between different texts by the same author. However, some writers are quite prolific and will have published more than one book or article in the same year. If you reference more than one piece of work which has been published by the same author *in the same year*, then you should distinguish between them in your bibliography by adding a,b,c and so on after the year of publication, you should cite the year **and** the letter you have allocated to the work, when you cite within your text, e.g. (Evans 1994c, King 2002a).

210

How to cite two or more authors

If there are two authors, you should cite both, in the order in which they are placed in your bibliography, as in the following (Evans and King 1999). If there are more than two authors you can use the abbreviation **et al**. (which is Latin for 'and others'). So your reference might be to (King et al. 2000). However, in the bibliography **all** the authors should be fully listed.

How to cite authors with the same surname

You would generally only cite the author's surname without giving initials in your text, but if you have referenced two Kings in your bibliography **and** you have referenced work which was published in the same year, then you will have to distinguish each by giving the initial too, as in (King D. 1998, King K. 1998).

The style of citations

Citations within your text should be as simple and unobtrusive as possible. Although it is absolutely necessary to cite your sources, you do not want these citations to get in the way of your own developing argument.

Example 1

Research suggests that people look for similarity across cyberspace, rather than an opportunity to engage with difference, indeed it has been suggested that usenet newsgroups and listservs, in particular, foster very specialised and limited contacts and discourage discussions that fall outside their specialised subject area (Kraut et al 2002).

Example 2

Longan (2001) looked at newsgroups hosted on a number of community networks in the United States, he found the same tendency to overly criticise other people's ideas and of the Seattle Community Network, he wrote that their newsgroups were dominated by very few participants and, furthermore, that many messages constituted 'flames' on individual network members.

If you are referencing more than one work from an author and each has the same year of publication you should distinguish them by adding a letter after the date, for example (2002a) and (2002b).

What happens if you don't reference your sources?

If you do not reference your sources properly, you can be accused of *PLAGIARISM*. This is always a serious accusation and you must avoid it at all cost. Plagiarism is considered to be the stealing of other people's ideas, whether intentional or unintentional. Plagiarism is always frowned upon and in some institutions it can mean that you will receive a zero mark for your work.

AVOID PLAGIARISM!

Plagiarism is *cheating*. It means copying or closely paraphrasing someone else's work, published or not, without any acknowledgement. It is theft – you are stealing someone else's ideas and work. It is also fraud – you are pretending someone else's work is your own. **Plagiarism is a serious offence and as well as receiving a zero mark you could be asked to leave the course or (if it is discovered at the end of your course) you may not be awarded a degree.**

Tutors know how undergraduates write and can easily tell when something has been copied and, because they read the same books and articles as their students, they can usually track down the source.

Universities now also have access to software which can detect whether something has been copied from the web and software which can compare the work of two or more students to detect collusion.

SO – BE WARNED!

TOP TIP

If in doubt reference your source.

Afterthoughts

So now you have come to the end of *Studying Society* and, as we have argued earlier in the text, it is important for us to conclude our work. Of course if you have taken our advice you may well be reading this conclusion without having read the rest of the book from cover to cover. So we will recap and restate the significance of this particular guide to learning and what we have set out to achieve through this work.

To begin. Both of us have taught at undergraduate and postgraduate level in British universities for many years. In addition, we have both been actively engaged in research – although in very different areas and with quite different perspectives – both in Britain and in the United States. This book, then, has grown out of our own experiences – as university lecturers and as researchers in both academic and policy contexts – and is informed by these many years of active engagement in teaching and learning. During this time we have ourselves struggled to find the best ways of doing research. We wrote books, reports and journal articles and modified these in the light of reviewers' comments, we studied different research methodologies and we grappled with theory in our specific areas of research. Some years down the line, however, we recognised the importance of the integration of all these skills for academic study. We learned, the hard way, the intellectual craft of the 'sociologist'. This book tries to give the reader the benefit of our experience and learning so that anyone who uses this book as a tool to guide their own thinking and research practices will learn the intellectual and practical skills needed to study society in a much smoother and more efficient way.

So this book starts with looking at ways which the student of society has to develop ways of thinking and studying which do not rely on textbooks or on the guidance of teachers but which allow you to branch out into your own intellectual endeavours, to forge new paths and to stimulate your own ideas and understandings. It then goes on in Part II to key students into existing sources of understanding and data and how to make the best of what is already available. Part III is where we present our own 'tricks of the trade', where we outline some of the techniques which we have found most important in our own research work – we look at how to search the library, the Internet, how to track searches, make notes and read for academic study.

We also introduce the important skill of evaluating every idea, theory and source of information which you read and encounter in the course of your study. Part IV looks at how theory and research are intimately related, how the student of society can use theory and how they can use research. We outline how different theoretical perspectives can be used to enlighten study and argue that without theory, research, study and writing about society lacks meaning and significance. Finally in Part V we begin to look at how the student can use their ideas and research to really begin to contribute to the sum of knowledge in society by communicating their knowledge and ideas to an audience, whether this be through the written or spoken word, through traditional media or more cutting edge technologies.

We hope that through using the tool of *Studying Society*, you will learn more easily and quickly how to question the social world around you and the academic's contribution to our understanding of that world. We hope that you will, in turn, begin to contribute your own research and thinking to your chosen subject areas. And that you will do so without making the same mistakes that we did!

Bibliography

Arms, W. Y. (2002) 'Quality control in scholarly publishing on the web', *The Journal of Electronic Publishing*, 8, 1: http://www.press.umich.edu/jep/08–01/arms.html [Accessed 19 February 2005].

Becker, H. S. (1963) *Outsiders: Studies in the Sociology of Deviance*. New York: Free Press.

Berger, P. (1963) *Invitation to Sociology*. Harmondsworth, Middlesex: Penguin.

Bogdan, R. (1974) *Being Different, The Autobiography of Jane Fry*. New York: Wiley.

Brooke, Noel M. and Parker, R. (2004) *Critical Thinking* (International edn). Boston: McGraw-Hill.

Burgess, E. W. (1925) 'The growth of the city: an introduction to a research project', in Park, R.E., Burgess, E. W., McKenzie, R. D. and Wirth, L. *The City: Suggestions for Investigation of Human Behavior in the Urban Environment*. Chicago, IL: University of Chicago Press.

Cohen, S. (1972) *Folk Devils and Moral Panics: The Creation of the Mods and Rockers*. London: MacGibbon and Kee.

Durkheim, É. (1952) *Suicide: A study in sociology*. Translated by J. A. Spaulding and G. Simpson. Edited, with an introduction, by G. Simpson. London: Routledge & Kegan Paul.

Eysenck, H. (1990) *Rebel with a Cause*. London: W. H. Allen.

Fletcher, R. (1991) *Science, Ideology and the Media: Cyril Burt Scandal*. New Brunswick, NJ: Transaction Books.

Giddens, A. (1997) *Sociology* (3rd edn). London, Polity Press.

Goffman, E. (1959) *Encounters: Two Studies in the Sociology of Interaction*. Indianapolis, IN, Bobbs-Merril.

Goffman, E. (1969) *The Presentation of Self in Everyday Life*. Harmondsworth: Penguin.

Goodhart, C. B. (1991) 'Sir Cyril Burt rehabilitated? in *Oxford Magazine*, 70: 8–9.

Great Britain Central Statistical Office (2003), 'Social Trends, volume 33' http://www.statistics.gov.uk/STATBASE/ssdataset.asp?vlnk=6484 [Accessed 11 March 2005].

Great Britain Central Statistical Office (2004) 'Living in Britain 2002' http://www.statistics.gov.uk/CCI/nugget.asp?ID=823&Pos=1&ColRank=2&Rank=704 [Accessed 11 March 2005].

Great Britain Central Statistical Office (2005) 'Internet Access' http://www.statistics.gov.uk/CCI/nugget.asp?ID=8&Pos=&ColRank=1&Rank=374 [Accessed 11 March 2005].

Haack, S. (1997) 'Science, Scientism, and Anti-Science in the Age of Preposterism', *Skeptical Inquirer Magazine*, 21: 6. http://www.csicop.org/si/9711/preposterism.html [Accessed 14 November 2004].

Hearnshaw, L. S. (1979) *Cyril Burt: Psychologist*. London: Hodder & Stoughton.

Jenkins, R. (2002) *Foundations of Sociology: Towards a Better Understanding of the Human World*. Basingstoke: Palgrave Macmillan.

Jensen, A. R. (1992a) 'Scientific fraud or false accusations? The case of Cyril Burt', in D. F. Miller and M. Hersen (eds) *Research Fraud in the Behavioural and Biomedical Sciences*. New York: Wiley.

Jensen, A. R. (1992b) 'The Cyril Burt Scandal, research taboos, and the media', *The General Psychologists*, 28, 3, Fall.

Johnson, A. M., Mercer, C. H., Erens, B., Copas, A. J., McManus, S. and Wellings, K. (2001) 'Sexual behaviour in Britain: partnerships, practices, and HIV risk behaviours', *Lancet*, 358: 1835–1342.

Kane, E. (1985) *Doing Your Own Research*. London: Marion Boyars.

Kelly, L., Lovett, J. and Regan, L. (2005) *A Gap or a Chasm? Attrition in Reported Rape Cases*. Home Office Research Study 293 (http://www.homeoffice.gov.uk/rds/pdfs05/hors293.pdf).

Leedy, P. D. and Ormrod, J. E. (2005) *Practical Research: Planning and Design* (8th edn). New Jersey: Pearson Prentice-Hall.

Man, J. (2003) *The Gutenberg Revolution: The Story of a Genius and an Invention that Changed the World*, London: Headline Review.

Marx, K. (1845) *Theses on Feuerbach* http://www.marxists.org/archive/marx/works/1845/theses/ [Accessed 2 March 2005].

May, T. (1997) *Social Research: Issues, Methods and Process* (2nd edn). Milton Keynes: Open University Press.

Merton, R. K. (1957) *Social Theory and Social Structure*. New York: Free Press.

Miles R. (1982) *Racism and Migrant Labour*. London: Routledge/Kegan Paul.

Mirrlees-Black, C., Budd, T., Partridge, S. and Mayhew, P. (1998) *The 1998 British Crime Survey*. Home Office Statistical Bulletin 21/98. London: Home Office.

Murray, C. (1990) *The Emerging British Underclass*. London: Institute for Economic Affairs.

National Committee of Inquiry into Higher Education (1997) *Higher Education in the Learning Society*, http://www.leeds.ac.uk/educol/ncihe/ [Accessed 25 March 2005]

Neumann, W. L. (2000) *Social Research Methods: Qualitative and Quantitative Approaches* (4th edn). Boston: Allyn & Bacon.

Ó Dochartaigh, N. (2002) *The Internet Research Handbook*. London: Sage.

Office of National Statistics (2004) *Focus on Inequalities*, http://www.statistics.gov.uk/downloads/theme_compendia/fosi2004/SocialInequalities_summary.pdf [Accessed 25 March 2005].

Office of National Statistics (2005) *Social Trends*, http://www.statistics.gov.uk/socialtrends35/ [Accessed 29 March 2005].

Orwell, G. (1962) *The Road to Wigan Pier*. Harmondsworth, Middlesex: Penguin Books.

Park, R. E, Burgess, E. W., McKenzie, R. D. and Wirth, L. (1925) *The City; Suggestions for Investigation of Human Behavior in the Urban Environment*. Chicago, IL: University of Chicago Press.

Patrick, J. (1973) *A Glasgow Gang Observed*. London: Eyre Methuen.

Payne, E. and Whittaker, L. (2000) *Developing Essential Study Skills*. New Jersey: Pearson Prentice-Hall.

Pilger, J. (ed), (2004) *Tell Me No Lies: Investigative Journalism and its Triumphs*. London: Jonathan Cape.

Plucker, J. A. (ed) (2003) *Human intelligence: Historical influences, current controversies, teaching resources*. http://www.indiana.edu/~intell/burtaffair.shtml [Accessed 9 May 2004].

Plummer, K. (2001) *Documents of Life 2*. London: Sage.

Roberts, P. (1999) 'Scholarly Publishing, Peer Review and the Internet', *First Monday*, 4, 1 http://www.firstmonday.dk/issues/issue4_4/proberts/ [Accessed 14 July 2004].

Robin, R. (2004) *Scandals and Scoundrels: Seven Cases That Shook the Academy*. Berkeley: University of California Press.

Russell, B. (1928) *Sceptical Essays*. London: Allen & Unwin.

Russell, B. (1950) *Unpopular Essays*. London: Allen & Unwin.

Smelser, N. J. and Baltes, P. B. (eds) (2001) *International Encyclopedia of the Social and Behavioral Sciences*. Oxford: Pergamon Press.

The Sociology Writing Group (2001) *A Guide to Writing Sociology Papers* (5th edn) New York: Worth Publishers.

US Department of Commerce (2004) *A Nation Online: Entering the Broadband Age*. http://www.ntia.doc.gov/reports/anol/NationOnlineBroadband04.htm#_Toc7802 0933 [Accessed 1 March 2005].

Wellings, K., Field, J., Johnson, A. M. and Wadsworth, J. (1994) *Sexual Behaviour in Britain*. London: Penguin.

Wilkins, L. T. (1964) *Social Deviance: Social Policy, Action, and Research*. London: Tavistock.

Wright Mills, C. (1959) *The Sociological Imagination*. New York: Oxford University Press.

Index